With Pen and Rifle in Kashmir

Photograph by Vishinath of Shrinagar.

MUHAMMAD GANAI WITH MY TROPHIES.

With Pen and Rifle in Kashmir

By
OTTO ROTHFELD

ANMOL PUBLICATIONS PVT LTD
New Delhi 110 002

ANMOL PUBLICATIONS PVT LTD
4374/4B, Ansari Road
Daryaganj, New Delhi-110 002

Reprint 1993
ISBN 81-7041-823-2

PRINTED IN INDIA
Published by J.L. Kumar for Anmol Publications Pvt Ltd, New Delhi
and Printed at Mehra Offset Press, Delhi.

DEDICATED

TO

MY WIFE

FOR WHOM

THE BOOK WAS FIRST WRITTEN

PREFACE

More than half of this book was written with no idea of publishing. It was meant only to inform my wife of what I was doing and seeing and thinking during a journey made in search of sport and health. The book is therefore without ornament or elaboration. All it can claim is to be genuine.

But the province of Kishtwar, situated between Kashmir and Chamba on the way to Simla, and ruled by H. H. the Maharaja of Kashmir and Jammu, is not only very little known, but is in itself extremely interesting. Its scenery is almost unique; its inhabitants are peculiar; its remains are undeciphered; and its sport is exceptional.

I hope, therefore, that a record not only of facts but also of reflections, not merely of sport but also of impressions, may be of interest, especially to those who know and love the Himalayas. And I venture to hope that the ethnological remarks which I have included may prove of some little value to future students. To the best of my knowledge no book has so far been written on Kishtwar and the only account of the country that

I could trace was a small paragraph in a large volume on the Kashmir State.

It would be ungrateful not to add here an expression of my thanks to Ramzana, the well-known contractor of the Amira Kadal and one of the few honest men in Kashmir, who made all my camping arrangements, and to Muhammad Ganai, my *shikari*, an excellent companion, who worked indefatigably in procuring me sport.

CONTENTS

CHAPTER I. PAGE

The Start—A Downpour—Achabal—The Kachwan Pass—Dyusu 1

CHAPTER II.

A Rainy Night—Gujjar Settlements—Gujjar History—Sir Walter Lawrence—Popular Gratitude—The Sinthan Pass—A Neglected Road 7

CHAPTER III.

Sinthan Bungalow—A Kishtwari—Dravidian Type—A Beautiful Glen—Wild Strawberries—Tsingam 16

CHAPTER IV.

After Bear—A Blank Day—Moghul Maidan—Chenab and Chandra Bagha Rivers... ... 23

CHAPTER V.

Katan Village—A Fine View—The Villagers—The Shooting Camp—A Leopard Shot—A Bear Seen 34

CHAPTER VI. PAGE

Recovering the Leopard—A Chance at a Bear—A Day after *Gural* and *Tahr*... 46

CHAPTER VII.

Conditions Needed for Goat-Shooting—Pleasures of Big-Game Shooting—Contrasted with other Sports—Effort and Pleasure 61

CHAPTER VIII.

Rainy Days—After *Gural* Again—Kishtwari Grass-shoes—Manners and Customs of the People—Their Gentlemanliness 73

CHAPTER IX.

After *Gural* Again—Their Appearance—A Miss—Looking for *Tahr*—A Difficult Climb ... 85

CHAPTER X.

Fever—A Beat for Bear—Another Panther Killed—I Try for a Third Panther—Sunshine and Rain 94

CHAPTER XI.

A New Camp—A *Tahr* Killed—A Difficult Descent—Another *Gural* 106

CHAPTER XII.

The Ramzan 'Id—The Moon Not Seen—Kashmiri Superstition 114

CHAPTER XIII. PAGE

Looking for *Tahr*—Buffaloes in the Mountains—More Rain—Moving Camp—An Impression of the Mountains 120

CHAPTER XIV.

Change of Climate—A Bear Seen—I Move Camp—Sporting Superstitions 128

CHAPTER XV.

Sitting up for Bear—Three Fruitless Beats—A Bad Climb—Fatigue—A Kishtwari Glossary. 136

CHAPTER XVI.

Shooting in Kishtwar—The Best Season—The Return March—The Evil Eye—A Hot March—Tugud 144

CHAPTER XVII.

A Vishnu Temple—Antique Wells—Kishtwari Head-Gear—A Hot Night—A Tiring March—Singpur—Camp on the Pass 153

CHAPTER XVIII.

The Girvit Pass—Compared to the Sinthan Pass · A Snow-Bridge—Sinzai Village—Fish at Wayul—Camp at Kandwara 163

CHAPTER XIX.

Two Days' Beats—Return to Kanbal—Back in the House-Boat 171

LIST OF ILLUSTRATIONS

MUHAMMAD GANAI WITH MY TROPHIES ...	*Frontispiece.*
	FACING PAGE
THE ASCENT TO PAHLMA	33
THE TOWN OF KISHTWAR	37
BELOW PAHLMA	78
A GORGE ON THE CHANDRA-BHAGA	106
KISHTWARI WOMEN	156

CHAPTER I.

THE START—A DOWNPOUR—ACHABAL—THE KACHWAN PASS—DYUSU.

I STARTED to-day, the 30th of June, on my long-proposed journey to Kishtwar in, I must say, the least genial weather that ever greeted eager traveller. I was roused (by the simultaneous sounds of my *shikari's* discreet cough and the less courteous bark of my spaniel) in my little camp at Kanbal on the Jhelum river at the quite awful and to me unusual hour of half past five (standard time, mind you, so that while it was really half past five at that moment on some fetid and broiling rice-swamp in Madras, 'twas but ten minutes to five or thereabouts in Kashmir by the still absent sun)—I was roused, I say, to look upon a lowering, leaden sky of unbroken cloud, dark, disheartening and dull like a Paisley Sabbath. Yet the clouds, or rather the cloud—for it was one and all-embracing—stood still and motionless; and I tried to hope, as I did my cheerless dressing, that the sun might yet air the day. I was in suspense, however, only until, by a resolve built on the futile hope, the tents were struck and rolled, the little kit packed in the leather-covered cane-baskets that are known as *kiltas* in Kashmir, and the pack-horses (so must I call them, for whoever on this earth ever heard of a pack-pony ? but they were horses smaller than most ponies out of the Shetlands), the pack-horses then were caught and laden. And then (having so long held off) the rain began to fall, not as common rain does, but with a stolid weight and vehemence, as of the tropics and a breaking monsoon, anything indeed rather than the ordinary decencies of a Kashmir shower or even what in this land might usually be called a downpour. For the rain in Kashmir, as in Britain, observes the proprieties, even if a shade too fond of an *obligato* of thunder, of a rather ostentatious, perhaps a little vulgar, display of its relationship to the elemental electrics of the mountain-heights. On the whole, it may be conceded, it has learnt its Aristotle well, at school with the clerk of the weather, and is averse from excess as from defect, temperately observant of the just Μηδεν ἄγαν. But to-day, on this blessed thirtieth of June in the year of grace 1917, the weather was averse without qualification in the French sense only. For the water came down as if out of a bucket, steadily, solemnly, without intermission.

From Kanbal to Islamabad, for one mile of made road, it was well enough. One could walk at least, and it was only, at the worst, knowing that baggage was being soaked and clothes spoilt, and the depression of the sound of falling waters, and the reek of unwholesome smells, and damp and dirt, and gloomy Kashmiris at the doors wrapped tight in their dingy blankets. But after Islamabad, on the unmetalled road along which on fine days swaggering motorists venture to the eminent danger of their own necks and the frequent destruction of wooden bridges, on that road, save us all, it was a replica almost of the Somme mud or the clay of the Champagne. The feet slipped, in spite of hobnailed boots and *chaplis*, in a way more like the clowning of a pantomime than the gait of a responsible man at the sober hour of seven in the morning. One staggered or glid or half-fell from one side of the track to the other without volition and almost without knowing it. Muscles in thigh and loins positively creaked and even my shoulders, from some inexplicable jerk or convulsion, began to ache as if seized by a rheumatism. For all the raw damp air, the sweat streamed from my weary brow and even the poor spaniel, the partner of my pilgrimage, sat down in despair and groaned, or came as near it as a dog can. It was less than six miles on the flat to Achabal, the famous pleasure-garden of the Moghuls ; yet, as I be mortal man, it took me three hours to cover, and I counted myself lucky that I had not, like a devotional Hindu, covered it with their 'eightfold prostrations,' prone in the mud on face and knees.

At Achabal I gave it up. In such weather it were useless to sing an 'excelsior', while the recollection that there was a travellers' bungalow at the gardens was as tempting as could have been a bottle of the old College Madeira beside the great fire of the Common Room. I hesitated no longer but preferred the modest comforts of the bungalow to an obstinate persistence in my intention—with wet clothes and a soaked canvas stretched above thick mud as my prize at the finish. By ten-thirty I had been welcomed by the presiding genius of

Achabal, the great Samad Khan, eighty-five years old and looking fifty to a day, debonair, with a goodly but not excessive corporation, the friend of subalterns and viceroys ; and by ten-thirty-five I had my wet clothes and sheets and pillows, and heaven alone knows what, drying before a generous woodfire in the bungalow. By tea-time in the afternoon the rain stopped and the sun was kind and I again saw the beautiful gardens and waterfalls and saw too what was even more welcome, that the roads were drying fast and the surface less like a patent fly-catcher. When even the stars came out at sunset, I felt I could go to bed at peace with the world and repeat a *Te Deum Laudamus.*

The next morning, the 1st of July, was by no means promising. The sky was again overcast with misty clouds that clung low to the sides of hill and mountain ; and, worst of all, old Samad Khan with more than three-quarters of a century's experience was at my side with evil prophecies of a speedy fall. But for once I hoped the old fellow might be wrong. I hailed from Scotland after all and the day seemed to me just like those mists of the Highlands which so often pass without breaking and clear away at midday to a glorious sunny autumn evening. The most, I hoped, we should have to fear would be a little drizzle, a " Scotch mist," which on the march might be rather pleasant than otherwise. In any case it would never do to be put off another day. The mountain goats, I thought, and the bears were calling at the other end and it was well to move on quickly.

So a level march of three miles brought me to Kothair, a pretty little village on a slight eminence. A little before, I passed the camp of a battalion of State infantry and a squadron of Kashmir lancers. They were in line, standing easy, on the parade-ground, waiting for an Inspecting Officer, when I passed. He had arrived, I could make out from the sounds, as I breasted the slope on which Kothair is built. It was curious, as it was also friendly and touching, to hear the pipes, in Kashmir here before native regiments, skirl out the tune of "Bonny Dundee" to the glen and hills, as if to Highlanders in another hemisphere drawn up for the charge on their own heath. And here, too, the glens and hills were almost, line for line, the image of Deeside. The *deodars* were the fir-trees, and between the forest-clad hills were fertile valleys, and the mists were the mists of Scotland. I thought of Aberdeenshire and the dear old "Doctor," the Laird in whose hospitable home I had enjoyed such similar scenes, and with whom and his kind-hearted cheery painter brother and the jolly guests with whom the old mansion of the chief of the clan was always filled, I had helped to shoot his grouse and partridges. *Ehen fugaces*! Between those memories and the Kishtwar road lay the War and how many losses, and in that remembrance what bitter sorrow!

From Kothair onwards past the village of Andhu to the first pass at Kachwan the road grew ever more lovely as the valley narrowed to a glen and the glen to a gorge and the gorge to a narrow track over the pass. The valley was rich with walnut trees, which never before had I seen in such profusion, and there were apple-orchards in plenty, and willows at every streamside, and bounteous crops of maize, while closer and closer to all these riches reached the stern fir-woods and the pleasant gravity of the forest. The climb over the pass is mild and kindly, little more than a thousand foot on a gentle gradient, and I looked back at the top without breathlessness to bid *au revoir* to the "Happy Valley" of Kashmir, happy in its dirt, its ignorance, and its miserable livelihood in the midst of all the gifts that God could shower upon earth. From the top the road cuts downwards, in one bare diagonal, across treeless grassy slopes, diversified with wonderful masses of white wild-roses, to the *ziarat* or place of pilgrimage of Hazrat Sultan, the sainted king, set in a clump of poplars. Here, after silently asking pardon of his saintship, I ate a frugal luncheon and waited for the baggage ponies, delayed by a typical piece of Kashmiri intrigue, to pick me up.

Hence the road led through an ever more fertile valley, opening into various branching straths, remarkable chiefly for the astonishing beauty of the little village of Shutur, enshrined in a magnificent grove of walnuts. Crossing the Nauboogh river on a frail bridge, our line took us by a turn due east into the *nallah* or valley called after the village of Dyusu ; and, three miles up the valley, at a height of 7,500 foot above sea-level, we found the village and our camping ground. Here was the last Kashmiri habitation we should see till our return, and the last village of any kind till we were well over and down again across the steep mountain range that separates Kashmir from the adjoining province.

CHAPTER II.

A RAINY NIGHT—GUJJAR SETTLEMENTS—GUJJAR HISTORY —SIR WALTER LAWRENCE—POPULAR GRATITUDE— THE SINTHAN PASS—A NEGLECTED ROAD.

OUR camp at Dyusu was on the road-side in an apple-orchard and would have been pleasant but for untoward circumstances. In the first place the village-dogs paid the camp too much attention and, what between their currish thieving movements and the constant growls and barks of my own dog, sleep was for half the night made impracticable. And then by ten-thirty old Samad Khan was justified of the heavens and the rain again came down in sheets to a lively accompaniment of lightning and reverberating thunder. Damper and damper, colder and colder it grew, till at one I had at last to get up and let down the flaps of my tent. Through the open space the rain struck cold on my face and the wind blew in sharp blasts that shrieked from the icy top of the mountain down into the glen and straight upon the village. I got to bed at last, chilled to the bone and not too dry, to risk suffocation in the closed tent, somewhat consoled however by the billowing of the canvas in the storm, such that I could see gaps, sufficient surely for ventilation, between ground and sides.

In the morning, when I rose, the tents were of course still soaking, though the rain had stopped a little before cock-crow. Immediate packing was therefore out of the question and I decided to have some breakfast before we tried to start. In the meantime I enquired for the village-accountant whom I wanted to see. I had happened to meet his son, a nice smart Brahman school-boy, on the river in Kashmir, and we had grown friendly. So, when he heard I was going to Kishtwar, he had told me of his father being appointed here, and I had promised to see him, if possible. But, when I asked, the village headman or *lambardar* told me he was away, staying in another village of his charge. For a village accountant here, as in British India, has several villages to look after, while his pay is even smaller and the compulsion to take bribes even more forcible than it is there. But I had no time to wait till the headman could send him a message, and so had to content myself with leaving him my *salams*.

We got away at last from Dyusu about ten with a difficult march before us but with the clouds lifting and the sun coming out. Above the village, the valley narrows and the rough road on which we had so far walked lost itself in a mere trodden track over rocks and *nallahs* among the pine-forests. For about two miles above Dyusu, we passed occasional huts belonging to Gujjars, those wandering shepherds of the Punjab and outer hills who in the last twenty years have added largely to the temporary and even the settled population of Kashmir.

These Gujjars are, indeed, a wonderful race whose history has still to be developed by an Indian ethnologist. For their ancestors were after all at one time among the group of conquering tribes which recast the chronicles and remoulded the characters, the races and even the very features and complexion of the peoples of India. From the second to the sixth century after Christ these hordes poured forth from Scythia and Central Asia upon the northern plains of India to destroy the old decrepit polities of the land and establish on their ruins a new society and an alien dominion. In all those hordes of conquerors, no tribe was more powerful than that of the Gujjars. From them and their kindred tribes come the Rajput clans who have given its noblest princes to India, however they may boast of tables of descent from that academic abstraction, the Kshatriya caste. To them again, in their later development, belongs the religion of Krishna, the God of Love, the God of This World, Krishna with his loving milkmaids, Lord of the free northern tribes, those peoples from Central Asia who had once known and loved the Himalayas and who continued to be men and free and passionate. Krishna it is who is the rival of the gloomy Shiva, the stern deity of aboriginal India. And in the religious firmament of India it is Krishna and Shiva who now reign, one the God of the dark aborigines who preceded the Aryans, the other the God of the Scythian invaders who overthrow their polity, not the solar deities, nay, not even Vishnu, of the intermediate Aryan immigrants. From the foothills of the Punjab down to Bombay and the Vindhya mountains, all India as we know it, all India as it has been known for thirteen hundred years, with all its ethical products, its castes, and its constituents is the creation of these Gujjars with their kindred tribes. The richest province in India and the most social and civilized bears their name ; in scores of caste surnames they are perpetuated ; and, in the Punjab, Gujarat and Gujránwála and Gujjarkhán are memorials of their power. But now the name of Gujjar, alone and unqualified, is borne only by a poor scattered tribe of herdsmen, who gain their daily bread by taking cows and sheep and buffaloes to graze in the Himalayas and by selling their wool and milk and butter. In the spring, as they march into Kashmir, the dust of the feet of their cattle is like the dust of many armies and the roads are encumbered by their flocks. They are the despair of sportsmen, for, as they graze their sheep (and they graze up to the snow line), the wild animals are scared from the hills till they seek refuge in the highest and least accessible fastnesses.

It was interesting by the way—and to an English official in India, whose only reward for service can under existing conditions be the grateful friendship of the people, silent and unrecognized, it was also pleasant and encouraging—to note how Sir Walter Lawrence's name is still remembered by even the humblest peasant in Kashmir. For it was he who, as Settlement Commissioner, "lent" to or perhaps forced upon the Kashmir State, abolished with a great struggle the most iniquitous system of land holding and organized oppression in Asia and established methods of tenure and taxation which relieved the peasant and left him hope and gave him interest in his cultivation. Such a one said to me to-day : " It was Lawrence Saheb who first allowed the cultivator to keep something for himself. Before Lawrence Saheb came, we had not even clothes, for our crop was reft from us as we reaped it. Now we are allowed to hold our land and our goods in justice. How should we ever forget Lawrence Saheb?" And it is after this settlement by Sir Walter Lawrence that the coming of the Gujjar, as settler and cultivator, began in Kashmir proper. Now the Gujjar settles high above the valley, alone and independent in his own flat-roofed hut built into the very side of the hill, separate from the Kashmiri villages and away from too close contact with his neighbours.

But even these settlers ceased in Rajpartan meadow, two and a half miles east of Dyusu, whence the ascent becomes steeper and the forest thicker. Constant climbing for another three and a half miles brought us clear of the forest at about 10,000 foot, directly under the unwooded peak up which the real ascent was to begin. A rest, a drink, and something to eat ; and then we started on the climb. The so-called main road or mule-track which goes by a curve to the north and then turns to the east was for part of the way under snow and impassable for horses. We had, therefore, to take to the foot path which climbs up straight, shorter by nearly two miles but of course all the steeper. From what I saw of the " main road " later, however, where it joined the foot-path about half-a-mile below the top, it was in no way distinguishable in quality from the latter. Both are, strictly speaking, non-existent. Either is a name only for the tracks made by cattle and ponies following each other up the pass. But a road of some sort there once had been, constructed by Colonel Ward, and it is the apathy of the Kashmir Government and neglect of its subjects' well-being which has allowed it to fall first into disrepair and finally into ultimate chaos and non-being. For, be it remembered, we are concerned here with no fortuitous path sought by an explorer in unknown country but are upon what is the main route of communication from Kashmir and its capital Srinagar to the richest of its provinces. H. H. the Maharaja is a chief of ostentatious piety and his religion inculcates above all mercy to all living beings and kindness to the beasts of the field. His foible carries him even to the laughable extreme that unbelieving Parsi shopkeepers are forbidden to sell soup tablets or beef-tea to equally unbelieving European visitors. But here, at the side of this track in his dominions, there were bones in plenty of horned cattle and of horses to attest the suffering wilfully imposed by this Hindu administration : and I saw the corpse of a pony, about half-a-mile from the summit, which could hardly have died more recently than yesterday, a victim, poor beast, to the dangerous rocks after it had struggled laboriously so far. The climb was one which I at least shall always remember. One of my baggage-ponies gave out early and we got it up only by taking off its load. Then, after every two or three hundred yards' ascent, another pony, which had carried up its own load, had to be sent down again to take its comrade's burden for the same distance. This process, gone through every two or three hundred yards for the best part of two miles, took time, as can well be imagined; and it was uncomfortably late before the last of the ponies was safely brought to the summit. It was extremely cold at the top, especially after the heat of the climb, with clouds every now and then blowing past and upon us and other clouds in the valley below. The snow too was more dazzling than I had expected. One of my servants, a Kashmiri, went down with mountain sickness but recovered fairly well after munching pepper. Both my Indian servant and I escaped without inconvenience, though I felt a certain amount of strain, and climbing, even a few yards at a time, brought a sharp, stabbing pain to the lungs and an intolerable quickening of pulsation.

In the cold, I did not linger too long on the summit of the Sinthan pass with its 12,300 foot elevation, but, after one last look into Kashmir, descended a few hundred foot to a spot better sheltered from the breeze where I could gaze more comfortably at the view into Kishtwar. There the prospect was certainly superb, under a sky which on this eastern side was cloudless and clear, troubled and obscured though it had continued to be over the country of Kashmir. Fronting me in the far distance were the magnificent and lofty snow-mountains of Chambu beyond which lay the *urbs in monte* of Simla; to the left the inhospitable peaks of Zanskar; nearer, between me and the valley of Wardwan, was snow and a grand limestone mass; while to the right projected the limestone crags of the range I had just crossed. But most beautiful of all was the scene in front at my feet and to the middle distance—mass after mass of dark, fir-covered hills rising from a narrow valley winding slowly to the south-east, into which on each side I could see similar valleys opening in a sort of endless chain. At the end of the vista I could just catch a glimpse of a larger, more open space on which, I knew, was situated the town of Kishtwar itself. But it was the friendly beauty of the forests, the noble crowded masses of *deodars*, which after the bare slope and snows and limestone crags of the pass seemed the most lovely.

On the eastern side of the range, too, for all the steep abruptness of the descent, there was a soft covering of turf upon the slope and the grass was bedecked with thousands, millions rather, of wild flowers of every hue and of every form. Almost it seemed like a Persian carpet, not spread, for the declivity was too steep, but as if hung or stretched downwards from the peaks to the fir-woods like a curtain. One large clump of flowers on a bush was especially wonderful in effect, great waxen white flowers, tinged and speckled with pink, with a sort of exotic artificial look. As they lifted themselves proudly above the lowlier Alpine flowers in the grass, they seemed almost to be blossoms wafted here by the whim of some sensual garden god, brought from the luxuriance of a tropic temple garden to this incongruity. Yet they were beautiful with another beauty, as of the flowers of a richer civilization, fertile in contrivance for the lusts of man. And, by a fitting harmony, they had in them a strange poison ; for they were deadly to the grazing cattle, should they browze upon their leaves, and their faint cloying perfume, when they were plucked, changed quickly as they dried to a nauseating and offensive odour.

It was pretty to see how the sheep, grazing in herds up to the very summit, took care to skirt the drifts of snow and never by any chance crossed the line to the barren western side.

From the pass to the gentler wooded slopes, which meet one at about 9,000 foot, was a distance of rather over four miles and the descent was tedious and tiring. The path, such as it was, crept down a steep and stony zigzag and muscles of thigh and leg ached soundly, long before the distance was covered. There was difficulty again in getting the ponies down and they needed much help in the rougher places. On the way one of the coolies killed a snake just as it crawled from under a stone just behind my spaniel, a '*gunas*' of that one species of really dangerous reptile that is to be dreaded in Kashmir. From the bottom of the pass the track went down more gently between forests of *deodar* to a fine open meadow, where a tributary rivulet from the north joined the main stream which flows to the south-east from the watershed and where a few wandering Gujjar families were camping with buffaloes and kine. At Dyusu the village headman had told me that a bungalow had now been built near this meadow and camping-ground, which is known as Sinthan, and half a mile further on we found it just inside a narrow thickly-wooded gorge which twists round to the right.

CHAPTER III.

SINTHAN BUNGALOW—A KISHTWARI—DRAVIDIAN TYPE —A BEAUTIFUL GLEN—WILD STRAWBERRIES— TSINGAM.

THE bungalow at Sinthan is a small rest-house belonging to the Forest Department, built roughly of wood, rather like the picture of an American log-hut. But to our weary eyes its view was more than welcome. It was already seven in the evening when we reached it and all were tired, and it was pleasing to know that we should be spared the fatigue of pitching tents. The crossing to the rest-house over the roaring, tumbling torrent was by a giant tree which had been felled and spanned the torrent as a rough home-made bridge. We were met by the *chokidar* or custodian of this forest keep, the first man of Kishtwar I had seen, a dirty grinning, good-natured savage, in tattered and indescribable clothes, but with gold earrings at his ears and a gold signet-ring on his little finger. In one way at least he had achieved what anyone at the first blush must have thought to be impossible ; for he was certainly dirtier than any Kashmiri. All the plenteous streams of beautiful clear water that flowed at his very feet had never, it was evident, tempted him to the experiment of a wash. But he was manly and open and candid and he laughed honestly and frankly like a man. He reminded me of nothing so much as of Dougal in 'Rob Roy' and when I gave him a couple of rupees next morning as a small return for his services, his delight was almost as excessive and as fantastically expressed as Dougal's when he received Frank's golden guinea on the banks of Loch Lomond.

But to me perhaps the most curious thing about this cheery savage was (as it later was at the sight of most Kishtwaris) how curiously and unexpectedly *Indian* he was and looked. A Kashmiri could never for a moment be mistaken for an Indian: he belongs to Central Asia and to that type of physiognomy which has been handily but unscientifically ascribed to 'the Caucasian Race,' whatever that may be, and which in Western Europe is popularly spoken of as the Jewish type. But here, in my friend of the bungalow, we had the 'Dravidian' pure and unmixed—dark, the nose broad-based, the lips thick and projecting, well in front of the straight line from the forehead. He was absolutely the lower-class Indian as you get him from the Vindhyan Mountains to Cape Comorin and from Gujarat to Bengal. Dress him in different clothes and he would certainly have passed as one of my Bhils from the Satpuras. Later on, as I passed further into the country and saw more of the people, I was able to trace that the blood of the Kishtwari population has been much mixed. In recent years, especially, there has been admixture of the Kashmiri blood and in not a few of the people the finer lines of that race could be readily remarked. But, more than this, it was clear that from early and forgotten ages there must have been in Kishtwar just that admixture between Scythian and Dravidian, with perhaps also some tinge of the early Aryan invader, which has composed the types of Indian found in the Gangetic plain or in Rajputana. There were not a few, especially in the central villages and among the richer land-holders with a traditional claim to the name of Rajput, who had as finely-cast and as fair features as the Bhaya or the Rajput gentleman of India. On the other hand, among the poorer cultivators, whose true class name is Thakor though now they take and accept the superior title of Rajput, the prevailing type was certainly the coarser, darker aboriginal head of the Dravidian ; and some of the Dravidian features could, as generally in India—except in a few castes like the Konkanasths or the Madras Brahmans—be recorded even when other lines of descent were dominant. In a word, there could from observation be little doubt that at one time the Dravidian race—perhaps before the first coming of those invaders who brought the Vedas to India—had penetrated to and populated these inner mountains of the Himalayan range. Just as, in Baluchistan, that race left an outpost behind in the Brahuis when it receded or was reduced and outcast before the more civilized invader, so here in Kishtwar too, more mixed, less pure, an island or rather a peninsula of Dravidian people must have been left, almost isolated, while the plains of the Punjab were seized and overrun by other peoples with different racial features. This Dravidian element, never completely obliterated, in some places weaker, in some stronger, in many regions dominant, is certainly one which, by its persistence and its unifying power, does in some real, active sense afford an historic justification—hardly to be found in Aryan myths—for the claim to treat India, in spite of age-long differences of language, creed and constitution, as a unity and a nation. To me at any rate it was a surprise, but a pleasing one, to find in Kishtwar just those pleasant, homely, friendly features to which I was used in my Indian surroundings; and to find myself at once at home and familiar with people with whom I might have neighboured in any of the Rajput States where I had so often been a guest.

The night at Sinthan, though fine and crisp, was bitterly cold and I was thankful to pile on every covering, the more so that the windows and doors on one side of the bungalow had remained unglazed. A mighty hunger next morning was one result and I was glad I had decided on a short march for the day, a later start than usual, and breakfast before starting. The freshness of the flowers in the cool morning, the loveliness of the shady glen, the sparkling, rushing waters, the luxuriance of trees and grasses, all combined to make up a picture that I shall never forget.

Our road still followed the same glen to the south-east, and we were to stop for the day and night at the first Kishtwari village on this side of the province, the village of Tsingam, some six miles from the Sinthan meadow. The road was downhill all the way, except for an occasional climb to cut a corner or avoid a cliff; and for the whole way the views of the valley in brilliant sunshine seen from the shade of the pine-forest were ravishing and delightful. As we progressed further and further downwards, the climate grew perceptibly warmer and the difference was reflected in the plants and fruits. It was interesting to mark the diminishing levels by observing how a species of plant that had been in flower at Sinthan would be with unripe fruit an hour's march further on, with ripe after another hour, and was already past its crop and season by the time we reached the level of Tsingam.

Thus on the way, I suddenly startled the coolie who was carrying my luncheon basket beside me, by dropping on my knees and rummaging with an exclamation of delight in the vegetation on the side of our path. For I had suddenly seen some ripe wild strawberries and was at haste to pluck them and carry them to my lips. Soon all were plucking strawberries on the sunny banks. So far, in Kashmir I had seen thousands and thousands of plants but none past its flowering. Here they were red and ripe and delicious. And how good the wild strawberry can be, how delicate its savour, so faint, so exquisite, yet so distinguished, imperceptible, one would hope, to the grosser palate, valueless to the swiller of beer or amateur in whisky, never to be tasted by the unfortunates who make bitter Indian tea into a kind of soup or broth by the addition of milk and sugar and can enjoy the decoction, yet how delectable to any who has kept his palate fresh and had some guidance in the nice art of the gastronome. Even at its best the garden strawberry can never raise a flavour so rare and choice. For the garden strawberry is too luxurious in its riches, too forward with its sweetness. The garden strawberry is after all at its best when covered in rich yellow cream and further enriched with sugar. Its luxuriant wealth of taste is set out by the addition and is improved by the proud pomposity of cream. But the wild strawberry would be stifled under such a dressing, as who would mount a Corot in the solid foliations of a monstrous gilded frame. The wild fruit has only one perfect accompaniment, a glass of light pure golden wine from the Rhine or the Austrian Oberland : else, wanting this, it should be savoured by itself with only the merest dusting of sifted sugar.

Here, on the hill-side in the Himalayas, how good they were, ye gods and worldlings ! How far from the tasteless watery berries laboriously grown in the Chinese gardens of Mahableshwar, the best that poor India can produce ! The last time I had eaten, degustated rather, the wild fruit was, if I remember right, at Marienbad, eight years ago, when kindly Dr. Ott—most courtly of physicians and most genial of commensals—had night after night joined us at our little table at Klinger's for dinner ; and had held us firmly to an abstemious regimen (spare but then how deliciously cooked !) while he seasoned the repast with his friendly wit and recollections. A pleasant table, we three, with the Doctor's witty sparkle, and conversation from lively to severe, and literary and social anecdotes, and delicious fried *forellen*, and then the wild strawberries and the good Austrian wine. Never again, I fear me, shall we or any English men or women of this generation see Marienbad and the Bohemian mountains so pleasantly and in such friendship. A tragic consummation! If the great King Edward—a political genius as well as a great King and a noble—had only lived, I wonder, could he have kept Austria out of our war, so fatally inevitable and so necessary, with Prussia and the German Empire? or, having come in, could he have brought her out more quickly, once she had gained success in her only essential contest in the East, to leave us and France to have it out in our own quarrel, our just and needful fight to the last, with the *parvenus* Calibans, the barbarians of *Outre-Rhin?* But King Edward in any case was dead, prematurely killed by unselfish service to his people. And fate had willed that which was to be. And now the Austrians are linked, chained rather, to the savages they detest; and we have to be at war (not quite so bitter perhaps) with them as well as with their loathsome and monstrous allies. Heigho! from wild strawberries relished in good Austrian wine to all this bloodshed!

But here again the levels of the hill and valley showed their effect, and when we got down to the warm gorge in which Tsingam lies, the crop was already over, and the nice boy who, for a miserable present of a couple of annas, fetched me a plateful of the little fruit, had to climb some fifteen hundred foot to get them.

Tsingam we reached shortly after noon and camped in a sort of little island above the meeting of two streamlets, beside a mill and lulled by its clapper and the noisy howling of the waters. *ἅδυ τι τὸ ψιθύρισμα καὶ ἆ πίτυς αἰπολε τηνα, ἃ ποτε τᾶις παγαῖ σι μελίσδεται.*

CHAPTER IV.

AFTER BEAR—A BLANK DAY—MOGHUL MAIDAN—THE CHENAB AND CHANDRA BAGHA RIVERS.

EVEN before I left Kashmir, I had heard that the village of Tsingam is famous for its bears. Now that we were there, information soon began to pour in of bears seen here and bears seen there, of bears that ate grass on the hill-side and bears that plucked berries in the valleys. My shikari, Muhammad Ganai, and I therefore went out, rifle in hand, after tea to watch a clump of bushes of the wild berry (*Kulmunch* in Kashmiri) of which bears are fond, in the hope (almost the confidence) that we should find one for our bag. On the way we passed the village, perched on the terraces of the hill-side, beside it a small but graceful wooden temple to Sita and Rama, the faithful wife and husband of the Hindu theology, favourite deities here as in Gujarat. Here, alone in the wide forests of the Himalayas, the pathetic story of their separation and their wanderings in the trackless tropical forests of India came to the mind with a vivid force and reality and one could feel, as something real, almost, one might say, personal, the uncomplaining faith of Sita and the sorrows and fearful wrath of Rama. There was something fine in the devotion of these forest people of Kishtwar to the deified prince and princess, exiles, they too, among the trees and beasts.

From the temple the way up the little glen—the Bund nallah to the north—was beautiful as I have rarely seen beauty anywhere. There was more in it of matter for pictures than in the whole forest of Fountainebleau or than could be used by half-a-dozen Barbizon Schools of painting. The glen or gorge was but a narrow rift between two mountains through which a torrent tumbled and ranted and roared and reeled at a headlong pace, while the great rocks were clothed with ferns and lichens, and the pines and birches and mountain ash grew in luxuriant masses to the water's edge. We climbed up steep banks and down ravines, we crawled under cascades and crept round projections. For a full two miles we moved in beauty.

Then we sat on the wooded hill-side to watch the tree-less break-neck ravine opposite, down which a bear was reported to come each evening to eat the berries beside which we were waiting. But though we waited till nearly dark, till in fact long after the time when the animal must have left his lair on the mountain top, if he were to come at all, yet we saw nothing and had to return disappointed. But even the upper road through the forest, past clearings and isolated huts of the Kishtwari peasants, was lovely in the extreme, while the drop down to where we could see our tents below our feet, in the cool evening air, was delightful and exhilarating.

After dinner one of the local sportsmen appeared and beguiled us with tales of two bears in the next nallah, whom we could get by a *battue*, a short way up, he said and affirmed by Allah the Highest, the Resplendent, "with less of a climb than we had had that evening and with thin small easily-driven patches of forest, one separate from the other, for our beats." It sounded easy and, under such conditions, the bears almost a certainty. Moreover, we were a little weary of the march and a quiet, easy day with so good a prospect of successful sport was more than tempting. I fell eagerly to the temptation ; my *shikari* only a little more slowly. So I decided to keep the camp at Tsingam yet another day and go off to those easy beats quietly after a good breakfast about ten in the morning.

The morning was very fine and we started accordingly at ten. Our way took us first by more or less moderate going up the banks of the stream which rushes down a picturesque ravine from Pāmbar in the North. But still the way stretched on and we still found ourselves walking in the glen without beginning to climb up to the places fixed for the beats, until at last we had covered a good three miles—an approach somewhat longer than I had bargained for when the patch of forest was to be "near" our camp. However we began to climb at last. And then it most unmistakeably was climbing. The side of the hill was almost like the side of a house, straight up and down, and we zig-zagged across it like flies on a wall. We climbed and climbed, and the sun grew stronger and the air hotter and hotter. Perspiration dropped from our faces and shirts were soaked till they clung sopping to our bodies. Coats, of course, had been early discarded, but the prejudices of decency and the heat of the sun set limits, however unwillingly tolerated, to what could be taken off. Thus, in the heat and up this steep acclivity, we slowly made our way, stopping for breath every hundred paces or so, sitting down wherever possible under the shade of some kindly giant of a deodar. For a solid three thousand foot we climbed and I was by no means the only one that was at exhaustion's point when we reached the level of our beat. Luckily I had that morning put on the comfortable Kashmiri grass-shoes, sandals plaited of straw and slipping between the big and other toes. In shoes or even *chaplis* of leather I could hardly have accomplished a climb at that angle. Luckily too the slope, though steep, was covered with grass and well-wooded, so that it was all safe enough ; and it was only a question of fatigue and labour. There was no call for anything approaching mountaineering : all that had to be met was a strain upon heart and muscles and an inordinate perspiration. But it was the first hill in Kishtwar that I had tried and it seemed formidable enough—especially for a day of rest and quiet. I had still to discover that for Kishtwar this was a mere plaything and to learn by experience that there are real difficulties to be overcome in the mountains of this land, before the sportsman can hope for goat or *gural*.

Now, after the climb, I found that the forest which was to be beaten was no small patch or series of patches, as it had been described. It was a vast, thick, wide-stretching, continuous forest of deodars between whose stems grew an almost impenetrable mass of undergrowth. One could beat three patches in it or thirteen; but the likelihood of finding the bear in just those particular pieces and no other was obviously not a good betting chance. But there we were and had to make the best of it. After plucking some strawberries, I took my seat on a bare rock, exposed to the sun, overlooking a sort of circus, covered only with undergrowth, curving between and separating two blocks of the pine-forest by about one hundred yards. The first beat came from my right, took nearly an hour and was a blank. In the meantime, on a rock in the fierce sunlight with not a breath of wind and with thunder-clouds gathering in the distance to make the air even more oppressive, I had had a grilling, or should I say a broiling, that I did not enjoy. The second beat was through the forest block on my left to practically the same place and was equally a blank and equally depressing. But a hasty cold luncheon did something to refresh my spirits and we cast about for some scheme which might still give us a chance. The best seemed to be to try a patch at a lower level where the berries grew on which the bears feast. So we walked a couple of miles further to the north-west and descended some fifteen hundred foot to a nallah, overgrown with such bushes. By this time, however, the men were naturally enough tired and perhaps hopeless; and they beat through the difficult ground out of line and badly. The result was another and a disheartening blank.

We returned, slowly and carefully, down the nallah which was both steep and stony, and found ourselves at last in the main glen about five miles from home. The glen was certainly picturesque, but by this time I was perhaps too tired to pay it much regard, while the impending thunderclouds and the stillness of the air in the narrow cleft between sudden and abrupt cliffs made walking, even at this evening hour, hot and oppressive. A country bridge of a single tree-trunk—and not a large one—thrown across the roaring torrent defeated me on the homeward journey : and I had to get a man on either side to hold a hand before I could venture on the crossing. Sideways we paced along the trunk, as if we were stepping some madly solemn figure in an impish quadrille. However, we got back at last to our tents by about six-thirty at the close of a tiring and unsuccessful day, where I still had to face the tedious duty of paying beaters, not without apprehension of an attack of my family enemy, the *mala podagra,* which usually finds me out after too great exertion and too profuse perspiration.

On the morning of the 5th, the orders of the day were for an early start, for we had a hot march before us. Leaving Tsingam which, for all its laborious failure, I had enjoyed for its beauty and its fresh waters, we descended the narrowing valley towards the next village of Chatru, about six miles to the south-east. Finding some mulberry-trees by the way, I solaced myself like a schoolboy upon stolen fruit, and found it good. The first part of the road was still fair to look upon and, until we had passed Chatru, the march was enjoyable. But, as our level grew lower, the mountains that walled the river became steeper and straighter and drew ever nearer, till we walked as in a narrow corridor; the heat grew greater; and the view was confined within the limits of the enclosing rocks and cliffs. Here were no longer well-wooded cheerful hills with light green foliage, nor even the wholesome gravity of great pine-forests. The mountains were now gaunt and bare, harsh in colour and in line, their only covering sparse thorny dwarfed trees of the Alpine oak. Stunted and gnarled, their thorny leaves of a dark lustreless green, these oaks leave on the vision an impress of gloom and inaffaceable melancholy, like mourners alone left to bewail the more splendid forests of which their mountain homes have been bereft by man's prodigal destruction. For, though on the higher altitudes the deodar forests have been left standing, yet, wherever transport was easy and cutting profitable, on all the lower slopes that are near the rivers, tree-growth has been stripped and destroyed with a stupid and afflicting indifference to the future. The people are too ignorant to guess what the results must be in erosion and the deterioration of the soil; while, in the past at any rate, the State has been careless and apathetic. The Forest Department, which has recently been established, may in time be able to do something to prevent further ruin and perhaps even to secure fresh afforestation and a new growth on the devastated hills. But the freedom still allowed to graziers to kill the new shoots by taking cattle and even goats to browze wherever they please, and the constant marks of the unchecked ravages of fire in these forests, which are everywhere to be observed, seem to afford little hope of real improvement under existing conditions. As, however, these forests grow in the catchment areas of the great rivers that water the Panjab and their destruction or even diminution will affect the irrigation on which that populous province must depend, the question of their conservancy should have a very strong and direct interest for the Government of India and it may be hoped that its powerful influence will not fail to support the efforts of the Kashmir Forest Department.

As they now are, these gorges are certainly wild and one at least had in it the elements of the sublime ; but they were cruel and inhuman, stark and gaunt. The camping-place for which we were making, eleven miles from Tsingam, bears the high-sounding name of Moghul Maidan, the field of the Moghuls, and it has been written that some two hundred years ago a couple of companies of the soldiers of the Great Moghul from Delhi were here cut up by the hill Rajputs of Raja Bhagwàn Sing, the tribal ruler of Kishtwar. But the local populace has woven no legend round the name, and oral tradition, that perjured jade, is for once silent here. The place looks at least as if made for massacres and cruel death. Here should be grinning spectres and dreadful apparitions of the lost. It is but a scrap of flat earth, torn from the restless river, at a corner of three gorges, shut off from the open air and from open view by rugged crags and misshapen precipices. The eye cannot reach above a hundred yards in any quarter, except overhead into the empyrean, whence the pitiless sun strikes his shaft straight down upon this devil's cauldron. The very trees, such as they are, are twisted and stunted and the air seems fetid and pestiferous. Two ravens which croaked beside my tent were the fitting inhabitants of this field—of evil jinns rather than Moghuls. The very coolies who had come with me from Kashmir called it to its face Jahannum, as who should say Gehenna.

After a slight shower of rain at night, we left Moghul Maidan next morning (the 6th of July), with little sorrow or repining, to face another hot and trying march. For more than three miles the scenery was a mere continuation of what yesterday we had met after Chatru, stark, gloomy, and monotonous. Then came the confluence of the Wardwan river with the stream beside which we had walked from Sinthan. Combined they flow for two miles to another confluence at the corner of the Kishtwar plateau, where their volume is further swelled by the joining of the waters of the Chandra-Bagha river. Below this confluence, the river with its mighty flow downwards though the outer barrier of the Himalayas is known as the Chenab, one of those five great rivers from which the rich plains of the Panjab get their name. Even above this confluence,the local people, looking to the uniform flow and direction of the current, gives the name of the Chenab to the Wardwan river. English geographers, however, basing their conclusion on the volume rather than the direction of the water, have considered the Chandra-Bagha river to be the main, original stream of the Chenab. But the Chandra-Bagha, which from its source in Lahoul has flowed through Pangi and Kishtwar in a north-western direction, suddenly turns to the south above the plateau on which the town of Kishtwar is situated, and joins the Wardwan river at right angles to flow for many miles almost parallel to its former course in the united rush of the great Chenab. To me, therefore, it would seem more natural to neglect the difference in volume and importance of the branches and, as the local people do, to treat the river along which we now walked as the upper part of the Chenab.

At all events the river, here in Kishtwar, was only too congruous with the surrounding scenery of the gorge. Torrential it was and terrifying and its roar was louder than the voice of many men. But its colour was a dirty brownish grey and it had no peaceful pools and plashings, no soft and overhanging boughs, no quiet back-waters. It was all waves and rapids, all force and strength, all muscle, so to speak, without grace or smoothness. Its waves leaped over rocks, high in the air, with all the grey, foaming ugliness of a tempestuous ocean. And the sides of the gorge were, if possible, even more stark, more naked, more friendless. It was a picture of desolation, the very embodiment of wild ugliness, elevated almost to something of grandeur. For that there was in it what the romanticist poets of the early nineteenth century called a wild grandeur, was undeniable. They might even have dared to call it beautiful, in their revolt against all that was simple and fine and classic, all that was nobly human. These were scenes for the Neapolitan School and a Salvator Rosa, painting in the gloom of the Counter-Reformation, the days of the Inquisition and the 'Dogs of God', the *Domini Canes*. No! it was ugly, but those who wished could name it grandeur, in the same spirit in which Calvinists spoke of the grandeur of Almighty God, when

Photograph by Vishinath of Shrinagar.

THE ASCENT TO PAHLMA.

they meant only the detestable image of a deity which they had fashioned out of their own inhuman cruelties and passions.

We followed the course of the river now on the right and then on the left bank for another two miles to its confluence with the Chandra-Bagha, a confluence more open and less unbeautiful. A Roman or a Greek would have found the former only shapeless and repellent: he might have excused the second. For just across the Chandra-Bagha was the rise fifteen hundred foot, to the flat fertile plateau of Kishtwar, on which even from the bottom of the valley we could already catch glimpses of fields of ripening wheat. To the left and backwards, steep on the mountain side, climbed the path by which I was to find my way to my shooting ground above Pahlma. Plateau and valleys, rivers and gorges, all were enclosed and circumscribed by the straight-rising walls of precipitous mountains.

CHAPTER V.

KATAN VILLAGE—A FINE VIEW—THE VILLAGERS—THE SHOOTING CAMP—A LEOPARD SHOT—A BEAR SEEN.

FROM the bridge the upward path was stony and vile, with a vileness that comes of loose sharp stones which cut into the sole of the foot and yet give way and rattle down at the first pressure of the tentative step. The heat too was terrible, for the air was still and the sun struck with all his force against the bare mountain wall. One could see the very atmosphere quiver under the reverberation of his rays. The level of the valley whence we started to ascend was under four thousand foot, less by far than the lowest point in the vale of Kashmir, and the temperature was the heat of an Indian summer, with the aggravation of great stillness and the reflection from bare rocks. For miles there was no water to be had; and men and horses laboured and gasped, tired and hot and thirsty. My poor spaniel, with his black hair to attract the sun's rays, felt the heat most of all. I gave him what drinking water still remained in my bottle, but with hanging tongue and panting sides he flung himself beneath every bush and sniffed for the springs of water which he could not find. But, as all evils do, this trial too came to an end, and, after some three miles, under a gradually clouding sky, we reached the Rajput village of Katan to find the friendly shade of a large chenâr and merry rills of water running down the hill and through wooden conduits to the rice-fields.

A long, long rest, with cigarettes for me and pipes for the servants, gave us all that we wanted. A Sikh revenue farmer came up to demand toll for our crossing of the bridges and was duly paid; and one of the *chokidars* or watchmen, a regular village "blood," created an impression in a smartly-cut, dandified suit of country cloth or *pattu,* with neat Jodhpore breeches, a blue silk handkerchief, and, to match it, of all possible accompaniments, a blue parasol, like some *midinette's* in the Batignolles. One could readily fancy him strolling of a morning along the rocky little Bond Street of the village (for such surely there must have been somewhere to justify his costume) to be admired by the ladies of the hill on their way to work. For, alas, in Kishtwar even the most high-born ladies of the Rajput colonies have to work and work hard, not at shopping and the picture-galleries, but at transplanting rice in slush and sticky mud and at reaping and tying sheaves of corn. The Rajput Adam may evade the doom of man and be comfortably lazy when he likes, but poor Eve earns her husband's bread in the constant sweat of her brow.

From Katan, after our rest, a track led us away up the dry bed of a mountain burn, a very trying climb at this point of the day, for a couple of miles. Right up to our intended camp on the shooting ground we could no longer hope to reach that evening nor did the path admit the further use of baggage ponies. So we decided to stay the night on a little ledge overhanging the valley of the Chenab beside a peasant's homestead. The owner of the farm indeed was kind enough to offer us the hospitality of his flat roof on which to pitch our tents and make ourselves at home. But there were too many dogs in evidence and the probability of an invasion by innumerable fleas. So with many thanks we declined his ready kindness and took ourselves instead to a recently reaped field a few yards from his door. I had only just sat down and the tents were still in process of pitching, when a boy from a house further down came up to me with a charming offering or *peshkash* (as the pleasing custom of the country as of Persia has it) of a little wicker-work basket with seven or eight splendid apricots reposing in it on fresh leaves. The apricots were large and rosy and plump, and they were ripe and luscious and juicy. These were apricots such as one never gets in Srinagar or from the vaunted gardens of Kashmir, and they were, especially in the moment of fatigue and after all that heat, entirely delicious. I gratified the boy in turn with a little present and we parted, I believe, equally pleased with one another.

The best point in our camp here was no doubt the splendid view afforded over the curiously flat plateau of Kishtwar. Rather oval in shape than circular, it projects in a curve raised upon an almost sheer wall of rock, fifteen hundred foot high, from its base in the bending gorges of the Chandra-Bagha and the Chenab rivers. In the north the completion of the curve is cut off by the sector of a high and precipitous

Photograph by Vishinath of Shrinagar.

THE TOWN OF KISHTWAR

mountain range. The flat surface of the plateau, hanging almost like a bracket fastened to the wall of a room, extends from east to west between four and five miles and something less from north to south. Its soil is fertile and the tillage rich, and the plain is dotted with villages, each hidden in its own grove of chenars and poplars, of which the biggest is the so-called town of Kishtwar, now a decayed little borough of a place. What distinction it still keeps is derived from the residence of the descendants of the two vazirs or Political Agents, formerly imposed upon the extinct Rajput rulers of the place by the sovereigns of Delhi, and by the survival of a fine polo-ground with stone goal-posts, which in these days no longer resounds to the galloping feet of excited ponies and the crack of stick upon ball. Some distinction may now in these degenerate times be held to be conferred by the presence of a Tahsildar, Revenue Officer and Magistrate for the district. From where my camp was, high above, only some six miles distant from the town as the crow flies, though some eleven miles by the tedious road, the whole plateau is exposed as to the observer in an aeroplane, in a bird's eye view, with each field and village mapped as it were and plotted from the next by clearly-marked banks and hedges. The colour of the whole left an impression like embroidery of old gold, as the wheat crop which covered every acre of the plateau was now at its ripening point and ready for the reapers.

It was pretty, too, to see on the hill-side near my camp but below us, the large two-storeyed wooden house, with many Saracenic arches, of the leading Rajput gentleman of this region, the lord of many acres ; while further up on my left was a graceful *ziarat* or place of Mussalman pilgrimage with slight wooden pilasters and a silvered dome lightly poised upon slender pillars. To this shrine, I found myself compelled by the opinion of my *shikari* and the inhabitants to pay a customary *nyaz* or offering. Without such a gift they assured me, there could be no hope of beginning our shooting with any reasonable chances of success. And I could at least concede from past experience that sport was unlikely to be obtained, if the spirits of the necessary assistants were depressed by a refusal to defer to their prejudices and observances.

In the later evening I walked over to the house of the peasant who had, on my arrival, offered me the accomodation of his roof and had some talk with the family, though their small knowledge of Hindustani made any thing like real conversation difficult. The elder brother, the real owner, was now in his decrepitude and sat all day, a dotard, with eyes that looked without seeing and ears that did not hear, motionless on a rope bedstead with a pipe at his withered lips. The younger brother, who did me the honours, stood himself upon the verge of senility ; and most of the work and even management of the house seemed to devolve upon his grandson, a spirited-looking lad, the son, I heard, of a soldier dead upon the frontier. In regard to management, however, I had my doubts, for the old lady of the house seemed to my eye to be no little of a manager and I should be inclined to wager there was little happened which she did not control. At any rate, as long as I was there, she kept popping in and out of the house every instant, and I noticed that she did a deal of prompting to her men-folk, the good woman. The whole family was cheery and friendly. But how, with their cattle and their sheep and their watchdogs, they could all crowd into the small homestead and still find room to turn or even breathe, would be a puzzle to any one, I should fancy, not bred in an Irish cabin. Among other things they asked me to treat medically one of the women of the house, a daughter-in-law they told me, who for two years had been suffering from a disease that she described as pains all over. They themselves, I gathered, thought of her illness in much the same spirit as in the *Fairy Queen.*

> " But this sad evil which doth her infest
> Doth course of natural cause by far exceed
> And housèd is within her hollow breast,
> That either seems some cursed witch's deed,
> Or evil spright that in her doth such torment breed."

But, whatever the mysterious agency to which they would more naturally ascribe these pains, they were yet anxious to try those European remedies at a Saheb's hands which they could not but invest with an unknown and mystic potency no less efficient and no less incomprehensible. As far as I could diagnose the matter, in my own want of knowledge, the poor thing must have been suffering from gout and dyspepsia, and, as far as my experience went, no remedy was likely to be of use except a visit to Contrexeville. This, however, was a measure that in the circumstances I could hardly propose —apart from the fact that the poor lady could not by any stretch be supposed to have heard the name of France. But it was no use telling her that there was no hope except in a long course of impracticable treatment. So, instead, I gave her some tablets of Aspirin to take when she felt her pains sharply and left her a dose of Carlsbad salts, to gratify the wish of all primitive people for something effective in the way of remedies. It made us all friendly and homely any way that I should give her something. For the Kashmiri (and apparently the Kishtwari also) appreciates asking for and getting medicines in exactly the same way as old women in the East End of London love discussing symptoms of their ailments, without prejudice or purpose, just for the sake of the human touch of sympathy and gossip.

Next day, after a clear star-lit night, a short climb of two hours brought us to our intended camp on the shooting-ground. This time tents and kit were carried on the backs of hill men, sturdy fellows who went up the steepest places under their burdens without faltering. The actual spot which my *shikari* meant to occupy we found already in the possession of a large herd of goats and sheep; while in too close proximity were a couple of lean-tos built by Gujjar herdsmen. Sheep-droppings and cattle-ticks are not pleasant near one's abode, however temporary, and the place, in other respects suitable and delightfully shady, had to be instantly refused. With a little search, however, we found another flat patch of ground, big enough for my small 80-pound tent and the servants' *raotis*, a little further up. It was not quite so near the spring of clear water, spouting from the hill side, which made the attraction of the place: but this difficulty was soon remedied by hiring an extra coolie by the day to carry water. Another disadvantage, which could not be got over at least in our lifetime, was want of shade. But on a hill-top I did not think this so material as in the plains and I did not suppose that I should spend many daylight hours in my tent. We were now within twenty minutes' climb from the summit of the spur of the mountain of Pahlma, at almost the last of the pine-trees, just under the precipitous limestone crags which surmount the whole range. To the east a path led, almost level, to the projecting shoulder of the hill, a steep grassy slope interspersed with great crags, which was said to be a favourite haunt of the *gural*, the Himalayan chamois. Bracken grew to a quite unusual height all round us and thyme and heath and forget-me-nots blossomed in the green turf.

After the camp was got ready and I had had my luncheon I set out in the afternoon with my *shikari* Muhammad Ganai and a local man for the eastern slope of the hill to watch for *gural*. To do this we had to crawl to a projecting rock, which looked straight down about three thousand foot upon the Chandra-Bagha river in the gorge below. But hardly had we sat there ten minutes when the local sportsman sighted a panther moving among some rocks in the second nallah removed from us. My *shikari* now conducted what, I must say, was a really clever stalk, leading me under cover crawling along the curves of two nallahs till we got to a solitary deodar opposite to and near the path up which the panther must come from the precipitous edge where he had been lying. We had done the stalk as quickly as was possible, if we were not to be seen, but we barely got in time to our point, as the panther was already on the move. I had never before, when shooting leopards in India, had so long and clear a view of their movements, while unsuspicious and undisturbed, as I now obtained. The picture was at once interesting and fascinating. The leopard moved slowly up the hill, lazily and quietly, pausing every few steps for breath and to look round, moving leisurely on as if thoroughly satisfied with himself and with the world, just like a great tom-cat wakened from his afternoon sleep by the fireside, strolling down towards the sunny lawn. When he came to another large rock, he rubbed himself meditatively against its surface for a second or two and then lay down on his back and rolled on the grass. Then, getting up with a spring, he again moved on lazily. By this time he was coming fairly near and might be about two hundred yards away. I, therefore, pushed up the safety bolt on my rifle. It shows how sensitive the hearing of the big cats is that the leopard at once stopped and looked round sharply at the sound of the slight click, carried in the stillness to his ear at such a distance. Seeing nothing of us, however, he still came on. When he was about 130 yards from me, he suddenly turned upwards to the right instead of following the goat-track to the left which must bring him close beside me. I feared, therefore, that he might go off across the slope of the hill at this point, instead of advancing further. And I therefore decided that, in spite of the distance, I had better shoot at once. Next second the beast turned broad-side on and I fired and brought him down. He rose again, however, and turned for home ; and I fired the left barrel, getting him in the stomach this time and again bringing him down, rolling on his back and, as I thought, dead. I did not even bother to reload quickly, so sure was I that he was dead, and to my shikari's whisper "give him another bullet," I peacefully answered "he is dead this time." But, to my surprise after lying still for a second, he suddenly rose again and made for home as fast as he could now move. I pushed home the cartridges in a hurry and fired and missed twice. But I had still time to reload again and I got him somewhere in the hindquarters with a third bullet just as he was disappearing into his native rocks at two hundred and fifty yards. As the last shot hit him, he gave a convulsive leap and cleared the rock.

The next question was what to do. The place he was in was a mass of gigantic crags with high grass and young pine-trees growing round and in the middle of the mass ; and the whole lair hung nearly on the edge of a precipice at the bottom of a slope on which only a hillman could move with any safety or speed. At the same time I was quite sure of my second shot and knew the bullet had gone through his belly ; while, as the first bullet, intended as usual for the region of the heart and just behind the shoulder, had not killed him but only knocked him over, I concluded that at the distance it had gone a shade to the left and broken the shoulder. Of the third I could not be sure but could at best hope for a wound in the thigh. And, owing to the war, all my bullets were unfortunately solid and not split nosed.

Everything considered, it was therefore clear on the one hand that in this place to follow up at once would be dangerous to an almost absurd extent, while on the other hand the wounds were such as, given time, must kill him and would prevent his moving. I therefore decided that nothing more was to be done that evening and that we should return again next day after breakfast.

In the meantime, we walked back to the wooded portion of the hill, a little below where we had been, to prospect for bear. Sure enough a bear also came into sight but a good deal lower than the nallah from which we saw him. Foolishly, in the excitement of a previous success, I let myself be persuaded even at this late hour to go down after the animal. The descent was through a tangled mass of thorns, without any pretence of a path, and to about eight hundred foot lower. And when we did get to the guelder berries on which the bear had been feeding, try as we might, we could no longer see him. Unhappily, as we were climbing down hill, the wind had changed its quarter and had in all likelihood carried our scent to him. At any rate, the sound of a stone dropping further up the hill soon showed us that master had quietly gone up as we came down. By this time it was nearly dark and we could do nothing but make the best of it and return homewards. But the climb back among the thorns in the dark was atrocious. I had already, at the end of a week's marching, had a couple of hours' climb in the morning, then the walk to the eastern slope and the stalk after the panther. Now there was this ! It is not too much to say that I was utterly exhausted and it was with great difficulty that I managed to reach my tent shortly after nine, feeling at each step upwards on any slope as if I were breasting a precipice. Even after a hot bath and dinner had improved matters, I was still thoroughly tired out.

CHAPTER VI.

RECOVERING THE LEOPARD—A CHANCE AT A BEAR—A DAY AFTER GURAL AND TAHR.

NEXT morning saw us out immediately after breakfast to look for the wounded leopard. I had borrowed a couple of dogs for the purpose from a friendly Gujjar and two more men also accompanied our little party. The main difficulty, I knew, was the angle of the declivity where the animal had taken refuge. The slope down to his lair in the rocks was so steep that I could not possibly move on it with rifle in hand and without assistance. I therefore arranged to get down first slowly to a rock on the other side of the curve of the hill, directly opposite the panther's den, at a distance of about 100 yards, from which I could reckon fairly certainly on hitting him, if he should come out and charge. Then the dogs, large fierce sheep-dogs, were shown the blood where the panther had first dropped and were let loose on his trail. The hillmen followed slowly, my shikari in the centre with my spare gun. They had clear directions not to hurry but to make at once for the tops of trees, if the leopard showed any signs of life. We all hoped, however, that by this time he must be dead.

But as soon as the dogs on his trail had turned the rocks and come to the hidden ground behind, their sharp sudden barks showed that the panther still lived ; and immediately afterwards, I heard a growl from him and a yelp from one of the dogs. Both dogs, however, after a moment's pause again took to barking sharply and continuously. I could, therefore, infer that one of them had pressed on too quickly and had been slightly clawed but that the panther was too badly hurt to move after them. The men had now at once sought refuge in trees as they had been ordered, and I called to them to do nothing in the meanwhile but to wait. For about an hour the barking of the dogs went on, interrupted only by occasional growls, till at last there were two very loud roars from the panther. He followed them up, however, by no other action. By this time, therefore, it was clear to all of us that the panther, though living, must be quite incapable of movement. My shikari stole down a little further and climbed a tree from which he could just see the head of the panther. He was lying in a sort of shallow depression under a rock, his head restless but his body immovable. The shikari then came back to consult me and said he could easily have killed the animal, had he not been afraid of hitting the dogs who were snapping at the leopard's head. We decided, however, to send off to the nearest Gujjar encampment for more dogs. In another hour half-a-dozen Gujjars, deadly enemies of the panther which for weeks had been taking toll of their sheep, came running up accompanied by their watchdogs. Once on the trail, all the dogs rushed forward and bayed at the dying beast. Even then he did not attempt to move. My shikari was, therefore, now able to reach and climb up a tree quite near the leopard and from an overhanging branch gave him his *coup-de-grace.* It was annoying that I should not have been able to do so myself, but the nature of the ground was too much against me. The animal was quite a fine one, seven foot long, and the fur in excellent condition, longer than is usual in India. The Gujjars were delighted and pressed me to try again for another panther which was also robbing their flocks.

After a short rest in the tents, I went out again about five with my shikari to wait on his path downhill for the bear we had seen the previous evening. The track was quite distinct on the hill-side, and I was told that this was his usual route, along which he always moved each evening when he went downhill. I therefore found myself a convenient place for sitting, about fifteen yards way from the trail. After I had waited about an hour, the bear suddenly walked out from some bushes about a hundred and twenty yards away above me and to my left, moving at a quick steady pace. I could have picked him off quite easily when I saw him. But I reflected that at the distance I might wound instead of killing him outright. I thought of the trouble given us this morning because I had not killed the leopard at once and remembered that the local sportsman who had shown me the bear's track had also said that the panther would have come quite close to me if I had given him time. It seemed also that the bear's path must bring him to twenty or even fifteen yards of me when I could make him a dead certainty. I therefore held my hand for the moment. But when the bear, still moving steadily and quietly, reached a *deodar* about ten yards down from where I first saw him, he suddenly turned behind it to the right, went above twenty or thirty yards behind a series of trees, through which I could just catch fleeting glimpses of black skin, and then rapidly went uphill under cover, giving up his usual evening walk altogether. This was a disappointment and a bitter one; for, without doubt, I could easily have got him, had I fired at once, and it was only the desire to make the shot certainly fatal and save later trouble which had kept me from firing. What could have made the bear turn his front, I was unable to conjecture. It was certainly no sound or movement of mine or the shikari's. The only guess that could be made was that he had perhaps smelt the dead panther's flesh, thrown down in the grass after skinning, and had greedily gone off to investigate. I cannot, however, say that I think this a satisfactory explanation. Whatever the cause, gone he was, and that I was furious with myself, it is needless to say.

Next morning—the 9th of July—I got up before dawn to return to the same place in order to intercept this bear on his way back, should he after all have gone down hill later on after his curious *volte face*. But neither did he come up the trail nor could we find any new marks. We could only conclude that he had spent the night on the top of the hill and had forgone his usual supper of guelder berries.

After a leisurely breakfast, I set out on the main business of the day, my first day after the wild goats and chamois of these mountains. So far I had only the vaguest notion of their appearance, their homes, and the nature of their pursuit. It was all new to me, very different, I could imagine, from any shooting I had ever done before, and I felt no little excited at the prospect.

A walk of less than 20 minutes brought us to the crest of the hill above our camp. We then began to descend a thickly wooded ravine on the other or north eastern side of the mountain, which was certainly the steepest declivity on which I had so far tried to walk. I had grass-shoes of course on my feet ; for in leather soles of any kind it would have been impossible to move in the places where we were going. The angle of the path cannot, I should guess, have been less than eighty degrees and at the bottom I could see it breaking off into nothingness between the enclosing walls of cliff at both sides. It was with great caution, I must say, that we walked down, catching at a handful of grass or branch of a tree at every step. When we were about half-way down, we suddenly saw some animal standing in dark shadow close beside the trunk of a large tree. As a matter of fact I should not say "we," for I was the only one who did not see him as he stood there. I could not find him while he remained standing still, though my companions, the shikari and the local man, pointed to the place. The local man said he thought it was a *gural* and my shikari that he knew it was a musk-deer. Now the shooting of musk-deer is ordinarily prohibited and is allowed only on a special license ; and knowing that the species was all but exterminated, I was not anxious to take such a license to secure a specimen. But while the two men were still arguing in whispers about its species and I was in vain straining to make out its protective colouring against the back-ground, the animal at last moved and with its movement at once became visible to my eyes. But he moved up quickly and I could not have shot him, had I wanted. Even then, however, such were the darkness of the forest and the deceptive colour of the animal, no one could be sure whether he was *gural* or musk-deer. Had we been able to see horns, the question would have been at rest. For the *gural* of both sexes have horns, slight and shortish on the female, whereas even the male musk-deer has only tushes and no horns. But the light made it impossible that even this should be clearly seen. There could, therefore, be no regrets at letting the animal escape.

The wooded part of the ravine came to an end a little further down and we found ourselves on its left or northern side, looking into the deep cleft of the mountain, walking on a narrow grassy ledge under the limestone crags of the summit. On the other side we were faced by an absolutely straight precipice of rock, unbroken perpendicular for some six or seven hundred foot. The ledge itself sloped down steeply, though not so badly as the upper wooded part of the ravine, and was only a few inches broad. To the right yawned the depth and emptiness of the cleft. To me, who have no pretensions to being a mountaineer—quite the contrary indeed—the first glimpse of the path was, to put it mildly, disconcerting. But, as I had to go on, if only for very shame, I at once made it a rule not to pause even for a second to admire the view—over bottomless depth and vertical precipice—but to keep my eyes fixed firmly on the footsteps of the man in front. At best the walk was trying and a handful of grass held in one's hand seemed a slight safeguard on a slippery slope with a drop into nothing only an inch or two off one's feet. It was especially unpleasant at one or two of the worst places where we had to duck under low overhanging rocks as we swung round with the ledge; and, though no doubt the humblest member of the humblest Alpine Club might have smiled at my fears, I let no false pride keep me from taking the friendly hand stretched out to me at such corners. The place we were making for was a sort of promontory, projecting over the drop into the valley, on the one side facing the precipice I have already mentioned and on the other facing a sort of wide circus of limestone crags and grassy ledges which here curved broadly out from the narrow ravine by which we had descended. We reached this point in little over an hour after leaving the wood and found ourselves some eight hundred foot below the top of the curve and of course several thousand foot above the gorge and river at the bottom. A narrow ledge joined the point itself to the main hill but at the end it broadened to a wide spur or space, six or seven foot across, on which one could sit or even lie in comfort. Here there were two or three good shady trees, one of them, surprising in such a place, a *chenar*. Thus we had beautiful shade and comfortable space for our repose. It was about eleven-thirty when we reached this promontory and there was no likelihood of any animal beginning to move till about three in the afternoon. On the way down, the heat had been terrible in the still air and on the exposed face of rock. So we now made ourselves as comfortable as we could. My men all fell asleep in a few minutes with that facility which is the prize of an empty brain and the absence of thought. This ready somnolence I could hardly hope to imitate but at least I did my best and rested with eyes shut for a couple of hours, employed with day-dreams and illusory fancies. Afterwards we all had something to eat and a smoke ; and by two-thirty we took our seats on a rock on the edge of the spur, glasses in hand, to search the surrounding hills for game.

The first sign of anything being afoot was, shortly after three, the sharp sound of a dropping stone from the precipice on our right. After some little search, first the shikari and then I could make out a herd of male *tahr,* four full-grown and one a kid, on the move down the face of the cliff. They were some five hundred yards away and the place where they were was separated from us by the ravine which we had descended, which was at this point impassable. So the interest I took in this herd was purely the pleasurable one of watching wild animals in their natural conditions, and was untainted by any sporting or murderous speculations. And the sight was wonderful. First, the coloration of these animals was such that it was almost impossible to pick them out when they stood still against the background of limestone rock, even at a known point through prismatic glasses. The colour varied from grey to a dark-brown mixed with grey; but all shades blended perfectly with the surroundings. Secondly, most wonderful of all, they walked almost vertically down a precipice on whose bare face hardly a sign of foothold could be detected. Where they had lain, I could not guess. Presumably, somewhere on the cliff there had been some scar or ridge just broad enough for their purpose, but even with the help of my glasses I could see none such. Now they were on their way down the bare rock-wall to a projecting ledge on which there grew a fair amount of grass and some bushes and from which a spring of water flowed. The oldest of the group was the leader; directly behind him the young kid, picking its steps with some hesitation and circumspection; then the other goats in single file.

But my attention was diverted from these goats by Laldin's discovery of a *gural* about a couple of hundred yards away from us and directly below. Him also I could myself see only when he moved, not when he stood "frozen" against the background. The question was whether I could make sure of hitting him at the distance and elevation. To me it seemed more than likely I should miss. For not only was the colour difficult to see clearly, but, in the position we were in, I could get no side shot and should have to aim at the middle of his back. I therefore suggested we should rather, if possible, stalk the animal and get near on his own level. As he was browzing on bushes in a small nallah, this seemed feasible enough. The only difficulty was to find out some possible way under our projecting rock along the precipitous slope by which we could get forward. But, after one or two vain attempts, such a circuitous route was discovered by which we could move down by holding on to grass tufts and twigs of bushes and by sliding over the worst places on our backs. When we got to a white stone, however, which had been marked for our point, not a sign of the *gural* was to be seen. The shikari crept still nearer to the edge and examined the nallah carefully but, look as he might, could not see the animal. But while the shikari and I, cramped on our little ledge, were still looking disconsolately at the nallah, Laldin, who had occupied the stone and was casting his eye on every side, suddenly whispered 'here he is.' I pushed upon the stone between him and the shikari, to find him pointing in the opposite direction. Here the slope was thickly overgrown with bushes three or four foot high. But when I looked where the man pointed, I saw the twitching ear and half the head of a *gural,* which was looking our way behind a bush. The rest of the body was hidden from me by foliage,though Laldin on my right could see more. I tried to push him along to make more room for me, but in our situation I could not nudge him hard and he refused to stir. It was obvious that the animal was on the point of moving and I had to fire at once or lose the chance altogether. I tried, therefore, in haste to allow for where the position of the chest must be, relatively to the ear which I could see and fired into the bush at that imaginary point. Alas ! and alack! whether I misjudged or whether a branch deflected the ball or whether (as I suspect) I had jerked my finger roughly in the hurry and excitement, I do not know : the one sorry fact is that I missed my first *gural*. One more twitch of the ear as I fired and the agile beast lept behind the bushes and was seen no more. After this miserable failure the tiring climb up seemed more fatiguing than ever it could have been, and, after waiting another fifteen minutes or so at our ledge without result, we began to make slowly for home. This time, the climb being upwards along the ledge and not down, I did not find it so trying to the nerves ; but, even so, I confess, I preferred not to look at the precipice opposite, which, though of course harmless to us, was by its mere shape alarming to behold.

All the way up the grassy ledge, we could not see any game, though we twice lay down and waited for some time in the hope of catching more *gural* on the move. When we got into the wooded ravine, however, and were half-way up it, my shikari, who was leading our file, suddenly knelt down and pointed into the forest and whispered, 'Look ! a *gural.*' In no little excitement I knelt beside him but, look as I might, I could see nothing. He tried in whispers to describe the place, told me to look for a rock, for the root of a tree. Still I could not see our quarry. My excitement grew more intense and so did my annoyance at my stupidity and the slowness of my eye. But suddenly, while I looked, I saw a piece of tree-trunk, or what at any rate I had thought to be a mere piece of wood, twitch and detach itself from the tree and move up hill. It was the *gural* which I had been staring at without observing. I raised my rifle quickly and, as I did so, his gradual motion became a plunge and an upward run, the animal going directly away from me. At the same moment I fired and the bullet hit him from behind, entering his thigh from below and probably penetrating his belly. Next instant, after a stumble, he was again hidden behind trees. We crept a few yards further along the track, and at the same moment the shikari and I saw an animal standing stiff and still against another tree-trunk. "Quick, there he is," said the shikari, and I raised my rifle. But, as I did so, it struck me as curious that the *gural* should be at the place where we now saw him. For, to reach it, he must have moved down and back a few yards, a very unlikely thing for a wounded animal to do. A longer look satisfied me that what I was now looking at was a musk-deer and not to be shot at. But now the doubt arose whether the former animal which I had fired at and wounded could also have been a musk-deer. But, no, his horns I had seen, I was sure. So the two hill-men who were with me rushed up the crags and found blood and followed the trail of the wounded animal. They came back in a few minutes to shout that they had seen the *gural* very badly hurt, making for the open top of the hill. They also said that the ground was impracticable for me but asked the shikari to climb up with spare-gun and rifle. But it was with difficulty that the shikari was hoisted up to them. For even for him, a professional climber, the rocks up which the hill-men moved with ease were far too much. I could only wait below while they went to retrieve the animal, cursing my inability to assist in such a country and my bad luck in having to leave to others what I should have been doing myself. While I waited, the musk-deer rushed past quite close to me and turned back again to the darker recesses of the forest. The men followed the *gural* closely for half an hour but could not get quite up to him. In the end they had unhappily to return to say that he must be left till next day, as it was now growing dark and he was moving into more and more impassable rocks. But they said he was so badly hit, that he would be recovered next day to a certainty.

This report was in every way displeasing to me. I have always made it a rule, whenever possible, not to leave a wounded animal or bird, but to try to recover it and put it out of pain at once, unless the animal were carnivorous and to follow at the moment quite preposterously dangerous. To leave a wounded deer or antelope untracked has to me always been particularly repellent. But in the present circumstances and on such ground, I could see no help for it and, regretful and annoyed, I found myself forced to return homewards.

Shortly after turning upwards, however, a stone was again heard dropping on our right. The *shikari* went to look and came back in a few seconds to say he had seen more *gural* and that, if I were willing to do a rather long stalk, I could still get them. We had both been disappointed so far and were unduly irritated and excited by my bad luck. So I at once agreed to the stalk, regardless of the fact that darkness was now fast approaching. The stalk was stiff and trying, at a sharp gradient over rocks on the precipitous edge of the hill. When at last we reached the rock that the *shikari* had marked for his point, the twilight was well upon us and every outline was dim and every distance magnified. The *shikari* pointed to the crags opposite on the other side of a small nallah and I strained my eyes for some time without noticing the *gural*. At last one of them moved, a fine animal I could see, at what in the dim light seemed to me about two hundred yards off. Now what I ought to have done and what I should have done, had this been a kind of sport to which I was used, the chase of the Indian stag for instance or the spotted deer, would have been not to fire when the light must make everything uncertain. But this was my first experience of these chamois ; I was excited ; and I knew that after a successful stalk it would be a discouragement to my *shikari*, if I did not take my chance. I fired and managed to hit and for a second or two we both thought the animal was falling. But he recovered himself and went uphill limping. I fired again but missed. Then, much lower down in the nallah, I saw a *gural* standing still. I took a steady aim, but, thinking that perhaps my former shots had been too low and more convinced than ever that the distance was considerable, I pushed up the leaf of my rifle to two hundred. A steady aim and pull, and I saw sparks on the rock where my bullet had splashed half a foot above the *gural*. I had misjudged the distance. And no wonder ! For two days later, I went to this place again and found that the rocks which in the formless twilight had seemed to me so far away were in reality only fifty or sixty yards distant. And I swore never again to fire in such a dim light, with a mental reservation of course for tiger or panther at a kill.

We had now to crawl down the hill slowly in the semi-darkness, disappointed and very tired indeed, both I and my shikari. On the way, in a momentary carelessness while talking, I fell over a stone and bruised my knee painfully though not seriously. We reached my tents at last about nine, after a day of ill luck, due mainly, I had to admit, to my want of adroitness in ground that was quite new and to me at least trying. Two wounded animals were left to be recovered and two others had been badly missed. This was sufficiently irritating, but I saw no help for it. I had a hurried bath and dinner ; and with my dinner I drank a brandy and soda, the first for many days, to pick me up from my fatigue. But whatever the cause, whether over-fatigue or the stimulation of the brandy or the excitements of the day, when I went to bed, I could not sleep ; and it was only after again lighting a candle and reading and smoking and munching biscuits that at last I got to sleep at four in the morning. The night, even at the height at which I was encamped, was sultry and oppressive, and the mist of cloud in which tents and wood were swathed was from time to time riven and reddened by the flash of distant lightning.

CHAPTER VII.

CONDITIONS NEEDED FOR GOAT-SHOOTING—PLEASURES OF BIG-GAME SHOOTING—CONTRASTED WITH OTHER SPORTS—EFFORT AND PLEASURE.

THAT the pursuit of the wild goats or chamois of the mountains is exciting, there is no doubt ; but the sportsman should be a cragsman born and trained, with a sure foot and a steady head, free from the faintest trace of dizziness or vertigo or alarm, when he creeps along a narrow ledge on some outlying spur of rock or sits on the brink of a precipice with his feet dangling over eternity. For myself I have not these pretensions and confess frankly to a distaste for sheer heights which clogs my movements on tracks which, if at a lower level and drawn upon a flat surface, I should traverse without difficulty or hesitation. Further I must confess that I feel that, in order to have any real success in this sport, I should be at least fifteen years younger. For, when the Aristotelian zenith of age is once past and the first few grey hairs begin to appear above the temples, more than all when an unusually trying climate in India, and hard work without rest for three and a half years in a busy Government office, have sapped strength and vigour, the mere exhaustion of hard climbing in the comparatively rare air of eight to ten thousand foot above sea level is apt to produce nothing so much as the *vanum desiderium* for fresher years and more youthful energies. To attempt the task without this steadiness and this recuperative vigour in full is perhaps fair neither to the quarry nor to one self. And yet—there is this to be said—that at the best there would hardly be any except the hillmen of Kishtwar, habituated to these heights and these precipitous rocks and acclivities from the moment of birth to the last *fataha* which accompanies the Mussulman to his grave, who could at any age follow a wounded goat to its last refuge or pursue him to his lair on the smooth surface of some vertiginous wall of stone. Then, yet again—as in most things—practice gradually conquers the first instinctive shrinking; and the place that yesterday seemed perilous, once traversed, appears to-day almost safe and commodious, while a more risky passage that twenty-four hours ago would have been impassable, is now attempted with no more, and perhaps even less, reluctance than the less daunting path which so shortly before was with doubt and difficulty mastered and overcome. And then again—the trophies of the game are rare and to win them tickles the tender chords of our vanity.

For, all said and done, all big-game shooting is in the end perhaps a matter, in the main, of human vanity and self-complacency. For it is the trophy that is sought and in its rarity is its glory. Did the actual pleasure consist only in the successful aim and slaughter, it must in and of itself be the same whether the horns be ten inch or forty, whether the quarry be a black buck or an ovis ammon. But the pleasure that the sportsman feels transcends the primitive joy in a straight aim and the primeval lust for blood and is relative to and coloured by the quality of his success. And this, what does it amount to after all but the satisfaction felt in accomplishing what few men have been able to do ? To beat a record or come near reaching it, that is indeed what is sought—to have attained by trouble and expense and effort what is for many reasons rare, there surely lies the zest of pleasure. An ibex for instance, in what way is it better in the mere shooting, than a blue bull grazing in an Indian field ? Yet to shoot ibex, not the young animal with a poor head which is rejected as soon as seen, but the monster ibex with horns of forty-five inches' curve, how much fatigue is undergone and how much ill-health and danger incurred in the high plateaux of Ladakh or the stony inhospitable fastnesses of Zanskar ? And at the end what is there except to lie in one's arm chair in the hall before the fire and look up at the head upon the wall—to remember the very place and moment of its shooting—and to recall with a smile how very few are the men who have been able to secure a like trophy of their sport ? This is, this must be, at bottom, the final pleasure and the real attraction of big-game shooting.

For, apart from such a retrospect, even the keenest big-game shot would probably confess or by a Socratic *elenchtheia* be forced to concede, there are many other forms of sport more pleasurable. For myself, I should without hesitation place far above it hunting, which is rightly king of all sports. The lovely scenery of the English country-side, the dew on pasture and furrow, the mist slowly rising from the coverts, the tingling gallop, the sweet music of the hounds, the lift of horse over fence and hurdle, the gay throng, the presence of ladies mounted in the field, the whole pageant in one word is an unmixed joy, more pure at once and more enduring than any other sport in the whole world can give. The mere memory of a day with the South Oxfordshire or the Bicester, in an English winter, will for me at least outlive a hundred days in an Indian jungle with a rifle. Pig-sticking gives no doubt, during the mere five minutes' rush, an excitement keener, as it gives a danger by far greater, than anything that can ever befall in hunting. But evén this excitement, greater though it is, is perhaps not in the same way pleasurable. The spirit is too self-centred and ambitious ; it allows no leisure for the complacent and observant glance for which there is time in the fastest gallop over grass. And the thrill is dearly bought by the dust and thirst, the heat of the Indian sun in summer, and the long and weary waits while the beaters enter the pig's cover. Polo I have to my regret never had opportunity to play, but it is perhaps rather a game than a natural sport, though no doubt by far the greatest of all games. But even of shooting there are other kinds which, for the pleasure they produce, I should put much above big-game shooting. A good duck-shoot in pleasant company on an Indian tank or *jhil* is probably of all forms of shooting the pleasantest and most exciting. Even a tiger, rolled over in full gallop like a rabbit by a bullet through the spinal chord, affords the sportsman hardly the same feeling of pleasant titillation as does the curl and splash of a mallard or a pintail stopped in its straight flight above his head. Next to it, to my fancy at least, comes a grouse drive on the Scottish hills in the purple heather on a sunny autumn day, with the pleasure of picking your bird as the line flies low and swift towards you and dropping him dead to the front of your butt or turning sharp round and getting another with the left barrel as the broken line flies away.

But again in both duck and grouse-shooting there are the other accompanying pleasures, the drive or ride out, the merry luncheon, the presence of friends, above all, the company of ladies. For, after all, man is a social animal and can find no full enjoyment where there are no women. Even in the grossness of the Middle Ages, with all their dirt and their superstition, the coarse unwashed boors who were given the rank of knights fought their tournaments under the eyes of their fair, if grubby, ladies. For civilized man at least, man, that is, as he was in the first two centuries of the Roman Empire or man as in modern Europe he has been, except for brief reactions, since the glory of the Renaissance, there can be no society and no worthy pleasure, no human and urbane enjoyment, that is divorced from the company of and cannot be had in common with gentle women. It is not necessary that ladies should share the pleasure wholly, that they should shoot, for instance, with the men. But they should at least be at hand, to dispel the heavy and fatal ponderousness of a single pursuit, to impose grace and wit on the moments of leisure, and to put men lightly upon their best and easiest behaviour. For this need of the charm and glamour of women's company is a condition of the civilized polity and the mark which distinguishes it from the beast. In a fastidious society, we may seclude our women from our pains and businesses ; but in our pleasures we must have them at our side, to give just the right flavour, the proper subtlety of perfume. And yet in England we still have to deplore the barbarous and perverse custom—now surely inexcusable in an age when men no longer drink and women most sensibly join in smoking—of separating men and ladies for a chilling fifteen or twenty minutes after dinner, to the extinction of cheerful entertainment. Here by the way is the chief reason why a dinner at a good restaurant is now so much more enjoyable than at the best of private houses.

At the grouse-shoot, at the duck-shoot, there is this added pleasure. But big-game shooting is and must by its nature be a solitary and a selfish sport. The object is to secure the coveted trophy for oneself ; and the conditions of the country and the game, the absolute silence required, the long stealthy stalk or the careful beat to a fixed point, are suitable only to a single man, or, at the most, to one or two men friends, thoroughly known and trusted. For ladies there is certainly no room (though a few of them do themselves shoot), and the danger which is of the essence of big-game shooting and its main justification should of itself preclude their presence.

But the worst drawback to big-game shooting is the :rge number, inevitable to even the luckiest shot, of dull blank days. Ah ! those blank days ! when from eleven in the morning till the late evening you walk through the burning jungle or move from beat to beat, tired, thirsty, hot and more and more despairing ; and never an animal is seen ; and the spirits sink, and boredom takes you as its prey ; and you come back dead tired and wearied, with regrets for a holiday that would have been better spent with your books, reading perhaps a favourite poem or some pageant of classic prose. And blank days after all do not end the matter. In small-game shooting the birds are many ; and, if one bird is missed, there are others to follow, and more chances to come, and continued excitation and a persisting emulation. The pleasure lasts and is reiterated ; and cartridge after cartridge revives a similar feeling and a further hope. But tiger or bear, stag or goat, do not thrive like quail or partridge. It may have taken you days of complete failure till you get your chance at all ; and then it is one shot only and the stake is played. Miss ; and your labour is gone and wasted. Hit ; and it is still one head only and one success, not a success repeated and renewed as in the tank or on the moor. Excitement of course there is, brief though it be, and an excitement more fierce certainly than anything to be bought at other shooting. In following a wounded leopard or in dropping him at the moment of his charge there is, it is certain, a stimulus to nerve and brain keener by far than anything felt in small-game shooting and approached (except in war) by the suspense of the gaming-table only or the excitement of addressing a hostile political meeting in a rough neighbourhood.

But it may be doubted whether the very poignancy of the excitement does not at times pass beyond the boundaries of genuine pleasure. You are waiting, perhaps, just before the charge or you wonder, while you watch the teak leaves in front, whether you are not being silently stalked behind your back. At such a time it would need at any rate a more courageous man than I never to feel a tremor which perhaps approaches the painful more nearly than its opposite and is at least situate very near that equator where pleasure passes to the antipodes of pain. At the actual moment, no doubt, presence of mind resumes its normal place by discipline, dispelling those nervous doubts and fears, and makes active only the usual pleasurable exercise of skill. But I should defy most men to assert that, just before that moment, they have never felt an emotion more akin to anything than pleasure ; and I should doubt whether there is any man—I at least have never met him—who would deliberately choose on any given day to be charged or placed in jeopardy of mauling, for the mere enjoyment of the risk.

What may be said and what I have sometimes heard asserted by the inexperience of youth in its novitiate, —youth well brought-up, mind you, on the best copy-book traditions—is that the effort needed makes the win more glorious and delightful. Glorious perhaps, for glory is the gift of others. But delightful ? Can excess of toil and unending weariness, exploitation of strength beyond its limits or tedium during many hours and forced immobility, ever produce of themselves pleasure and delight ? Or rather is not even the value of the prize, in its intrinsic worth to the winner, debased and discounted by all this labour ? It was, I believe, the commercial middle-class of the nineteenth century which painfully invented the theory that what is earned by hard effort gains an added zest and that easily come by is easily thrown away. Such adages must, I should imagine, form the filling matter for the works of the ineffable Mr. Smiles. But let any one of healthy, normal, sensual mankind look into his heart and speak the truth. Let him forget for a moment the groans and rebukes of money-making respectability. I think he will agree, if he be candid with himself, that it is just the things that he gained without effort, or with an effort so slight as to be pleasurable in itself, which gave him the most real and complete delight. It is the country walk at one's own time across the fields which one enjoys ; not surely the heel and toe pedestrian match. But in this, as in so many other maxims of nineteenth century commercialism, it is difficult to be certain how far the parrot-speakers were honest with themselves and merely self-deceived, how far they were consciously and intentionally lying. For hypocrisy was so far ingrained (would that the verb were finally preterite and not indefinitely continuative !) that the lie for the world and the lie in the soul were only too often indistinguishable, even for the poor twisted miserable soul itself. Perhaps—to deal liberally with such moralists of the shop and counter—the adage may have truth, if confined to the pursuit of wealth. For money in itself is so poor an object and penurious, its gain so trivial and worthless, that possibly the effort of its pursuit may have more zest than its actual acquisition; and the ethical perversity may at least serve as a consolation to the poor wretch bound to his office-stool and business. But truer by far, to living natural humanity, is even the paradox of Lord Melbourne, that the Garter was so satisfactory because there was no damned merit about it.

One is sometimes told that the first money one earns is never forgotten and gives the keenest pleasure. For myself, I am not sure now what the first money I earned happened to be. Probably, I think, it was a few miserable guineas I got as a boy of sixteen or seventeen for a series of articles in a Scottish newspaper on the Milleniary Exhibition in Budapest. If so, and I think I am right and those were my first earnings, I am sure at least that I hardly stopped to think of the money, but my pleasure was (for the first time) to find myself flourishing, however sketchy and tawdry a flourish, in public print for some of the little world in which I lived to read and recognize. Certainly an income earned in a profession or a service is always spoiled by the bitterness of the work given to its earning. Much which falls within the terms of work may in itself be pleasurable, if it be important and in harmony with some great or noble purpose. But the incessant compromise and that unpleasing routine, those dull minutiae which must also, it is recognized, be fully grasped and performed, those are a heavy counterweight to occasional satisfactions. And there is not a man who, as he stretches out his cap for his pay, does not think that surely the hire is not worthy of the labourer. Every candid man must, I think, allow that there is greater pleasure in an unexpected legacy or a prize in a lottery than in his monthly wage or salary. Is not the turning-up of the number which carries one's coin at the roulette-table more of a delight than the gain by harder effort of mind or body of ten times the sum? Nay, even in love, for all the words of the old and ugly and the disappointed, it is assuredly not the long courtship and the prolonged indifference at last overcome which give the pleasure. To me at any rate it would seem that there can hardly be Helen of Troy or Rachel of the Israelites that could requite sufficiently so long a service or at the last end be able to drug memory to sleep and to sweeten with her favours the bitter guerdon of wasted days. Life is too full and rich to be engrossed upon one single deed of gift. It has its other claims and dispositions to be inscribed upon the documents of humanity. So, even in love, flustered hesitancy there may well be and the brief resistance, resting on natural modesty and the coy wilfulness of young desire, which stimulate without depressing and enhance the energies without dissipating them; but they should culminate, not too unduly late, in the generous response and warm acceptance which fix and crown an unselfish and a wholesome affection.

So, in shooting also, it is not the long, tiring stalk, even if it terminates in a successful shot with muscles tightened against fatigue and lungs held fast for a second against straining gasps, which at the moment or in retrospect affords the greatest pleasure. Rather it is the day when, leaving your camp in the morning, rifle on shoulder, you walked within five minutes, without thought or preparation, into a herd of cheetal and bagged with one easy shot the stag with 39-inch horns ; or the evening when you had barely climbed to your tree over the kill before a trusting panther came out into the readiest line of fire.

No, one faces the effort for the sake of the reward, the rare trophy and the satisfaction that follows on its acquisition. But it is never the straining effort which is itself the cause of pleasure.

For myself, what in such shooting I like best is the view of forest and mountain, the stillness and repose, and the sight of bird and animal ; that and the self-control one learns to exercise over will and muscle, sitting silent and immoveable while mosquitoes sting and flies settle and worry, or when the coming cough has to be stifled. Leaves loosen themselves from branches and come down to the ground with a noise, in the jungle depths, like a pistol-shot ; butterflies, gaily painted, flutter-bye (that better old English word !) ; a woodpecker picks for insects underneath the bark of a pine-tree ; and the chikor croaks in the bracken or flies past like a bolt from a bow. In these sights and sounds, I think, is the best of pleasure to be found. And I often think that those truer sportsmen or lovers of nature have taken the better part who, at the same danger and with similar effort, snap an instantaneous camera at the crouching leopard or the galloping stag instead of the trigger of the fatal rifle.

CHAPTER VIII.

RAINY DAYS—AFTER GURAL AGAIN—KISHTWARI GRASS-SHOES—MANNERS AND CUSTOMS OF THE PEOPLE—THEIR GENTLEMANLINESS.

THE next day, the 10th of July, I had determined should be a day of rest, at any rate for myself. For I could no longer doubt that I was over-tired and that the long days of climbing in these mountains had taken too much out of me, weakened as I had been by illness in my last Indian station. A day with nothing to do except read and write letters seemed, therefore, to be advisable. As it happened, it was very fortunate that I had decided in this way, for a heavy thunderstorm broke about one o'clock and was followed by torrential rain till evening. The *shikari* and the two local men engaged by me had gone out in the morning after breakfast to look for the wounded animals. Poor wretches, they returned about three, drenched to the skin and weary, having seen the one *gural* and stalked him, badly wounded as he was, over the roughest of rough ground. They had got within twenty yards of him and then missed him with the spare gun at that distance. The storm had come on in all its violence; slowly though he moved, the wounded *gural* led them into more and more impassable ground, and finally they had had to turn tail before the elements and come back to shelter.

I was disgusted at the whole affair, and the dismal deluge and thick clouds, so thick that I could barely see the outline of the pine-trees, ten yards from my tent, were not likely to improve my spirits. My *shikari* and I, however, tried to persuade ourselves that the rain would have cleared away by morning and that on a fine sunny day it would be easy to recover the wounded beasts, if only by watching for the gathering of kites and vultures. I wrote letters for a good part of the day, and at night had the joy of receiving the coolie with my post from Kishtwar town. He brought the post which had arrived there in the previous three days, with a large budget from my wife and a parcel of books, how infinitely welcome, which she had forwarded on to me. On such a day the sight of Taraporewala's well-known name upon the parcel was like a tonic ; and I was unspeakably grateful to find, on cutting the string, five volumes of the Loeb Library, which I had sent for just before leaving Kashmir. I lay down at once on my bed and read Bion and Theocritus until dark, and blessed the generous millionaire—almost the only millionaire I have ever heard of that was any use to himself or anyone else—who had endowed this magnificent edition of the classics. Good texts, good printing, a neat and handy shape, these are all delightful, but best of all to any one like myself is the translation ready for reference on the opposite page, whenever one's obliterated knowledge of Greek stumbles and halts at a difficulty. I do not know if Mr. Loeb is still among the living or not ; but sometime I trust, in the Elysian fields, if hardly in America during life, I may draw near his pallid shade among the crowd of grateful spirits who have owed him so much enjoyment while they were alive and add my own faint murmur of thanks and praise to the general twitter of the dead, that speak, says Homer, in voices like the sound of many bats.

The eleventh was again a day of rain. There had been another thunderstorm in the night, and I woke up to see nothing except thick cloud and hear only the loud pattering of heavy drops. All through the day, it continued to rain heavily except when, for half-an-hour or so at a time, the positive downpour gave place to a mere negative Scotch mist. Reading was the only resource; but even the erotics of Theocritus or the burning human sympathies of Euripides could not warm one against the raw cold which rolled in with the mist and distilled from the soaked canvas. In an 80-lb. tent there is no room for a fire, even had the wood not been wet and smoky; and the wicker-work basket filled with charcoal, which all Kashmiris carry and tie by a string round their necks under their clothes and with which they constantly burn and scar their skin, was unknown in Kishtwar and unprocurable on a mountain summit, inhabited only by the beasts of the rock and forest. So there was nothing for it but to lie on the bed covered with a rug and hold one's book with one hand at a time, while the other snuggled under the bed-clothes to get warm again. By five in the evening, however, the rain held off for a bit, though the sky remained heavily overcast and the hills opposite on the other side of the valley were shrouded in shifts of mist. On the whole I thought it would be worth while to go out again to look for *gural* from the summit of the hill quite close to my camp. It seemed an easy way to climb from where I was and we should get above the nallah where I had seen *gural* the evening before last. But when I got beyond the wooded slopes, I found myself faced with quite formidable difficulties. For the last part of the climb had perforce to be over limestone-boulders, and the foot-grips between were covered with loose fragments of stone which yielded at every step. I got on well enough till we reached the rock overhanging the first nallah on the other side, where we ensconced ourselves to watch. But after waiting for twenty minutes and seeing nothing we had to try to move on to the further point, on the other side of the ravine, to search the larger nallah beyond. In order to do this, we had to clamber round on the top edge of the ravine, over exactly the same sort of stones, but with a most unpleasant drop on the downward side. Here, I confess, I took a hill-man's hand while we crossed and drew a deep breath when at last I was able to sit down on the opposite ledge. For all our toil, however, we saw nothing, except two *gural* about half-a-mile away as the crow flies, a long way down the hill, and about three miles away by the nearest track. It was, therefore, far too late in the evening even to think of trying to stalk them. What was of interest, however, was that these were evidently two out of the three *gural* at which I had fired the night before and of which I was certain I had wounded one. The third was, therefore, evidently either incapacitated or dead. But the problem was how to find him. For the rain had made the hill-sides far too dangerous for even the surest-footed hill-man, while the clouds both prevented kites from finding their food and men from seeing the birds of prey.

We returned slowly with the rain once more beginning and I admired again, as I had so often done before, the agility and sure-footedness of the Kishtwaris on any slope or rock. Their grass-shoes, as a matter of fact, are quite different in shape from those of the Kashmiris. The Kashmiri grass-shoe is a real shoe secured by one cord of straw between the big toe and the other toes, by three or four cords across the instep, and by two cords over the heel. It sits firmly and tightly to the foot. The Kishtwari's shoe, on the other hand, is merely a sole with one broad band between the big and other toes, fastened loosely at both sides to the sole. The heel is quite loose and unbound and indeed the effect is like that of some slippers or sandals used in Turkish-baths in which you slide from one room to another. How the men keep these shoes tight to their feet in the dangerous places where they leap like goats, is a perfect puzzle. But they told me that constant practice makes the shoes sit tight to their feet ; and that they prefer them as they are, because in this way they can grip stones tightly with their toes, which they cannot do with the Kashmir shoe.

I was called at five next morning to go out and try to intercept the bear that I had let go the other day. The sight of the morning out of the tent-door was enough to send me back to bed, for every blade of grass and every leaf was dripping and the air was again thick with rain and cloud. But, with the help of a cup of tea, I conquered my repugnance and set out thickly clad and with a waterproof over all. The bear was, however, probably less of a fool than we were and remained snug in some cosy bed of leaves. At any rate he did not pass our way; and I returned cold and wretched to breakfast. By nine, it was already pouring and all through the day it poured harder than ever. At last in the evening, as the only alternative appeared to be suicide, I took my rifle again and sat in the same gully waiting for the same bear with the same result, while the rain poured down and my feet, in spite of puttoo socks and grass-shoes, grew colder and more numb and the clouds tossed and rolled their grey wreaths over the valley. The main mass of cloud lifted a little at sunset and allowed glimpses to be seen of the mountains across the Chenab, obscured from minute to minute by the drifts of mist which rose from the river level or blew past from the lower valleys to cling upon the pine trees or cover the shrinking summits with an impenetrable veil.

The night was one of the coldest I have ever felt, raw, damp, piercing cold that found its way to the very bone and stung. Even with underclothing below my sleeping-suit and with rug and blanket over me, I still felt the cold bitterly and in the end found that I simply must close the tent-flaps to keep warm.

The Kishtwaris, I find, like so many other wild peoples, have the most curious and confused ideas about medicines and their givers. They come to me daily with requests for treatment for all impossible things. A man with a cataract, for instance, came to

Photograph by Vishinath of Shrinagar.

BELOW PAHLMA

me in all confidence to beg that I should restore his sight, and I feel certain that he put down my refusal to touch anyone's eye to some personal dislike or other on my part. What drugs I do give, they absorb with full trust: and if faith can heal, surely the pills they take from my hand should prove efficacious. But to a professional medical man they will not go. Kishtwar is only a few miles away, nothing of a journey to a hill-man, and in the little borough there is a dispensary maintained by the state with a properly-qualified Sub-Assistant Surgeon. But I find that not a man from here will attend the dispensary. One knows of course and regrets it, that even high medical authorities at home and in British India advocate and countenance, by some perverse and misguided individualism, the grabbing of fees by physicians and the sale of medical advice in a competitive market like a tradesman's goods, though the system is ruining the honour and status of their fellowship. I thought, therefore, that the reluctance of the people might be connected with demands for fees by a doctor, qualified at any rate to follow the example set in this respect by the heads of his profession; or else might be due to that not infrequent rudeness to poorer patients, of which I have seen only too much in India. But enquiry soon showed me that here, in Kishtwar at least, this was not the case. The sole cause of reluctance, it came out, was the deep-rooted fear and belief that the doctor would intentionally murder his patients. They really and truly believed that the main aim and end of a surgeon's appointment to a dispensary was that he should kill off as many as possible of the population. I pointed out to my would-be patients that, as these Sub-Assistant Surgeons were trained by Englishmen and their service devised and organized by them, it must evidently be equally perilous to their bodies to trust me or any other Englishman : or rather, that as they were prepared to take medicines from us, they should equally trust the professional men who were trained after all under our auspices and by our practice. One would have thought that the point would pierce the densest skull. But I could see that it made no impression whatever. They still stretched out their hands to my medicine-case but they still shook their heads at the suggestion of a visit to the dispensary. Is there something in poverty, I wonder, which makes men so perversely stupid ? Even in England in the poorer quarters one hears all sorts of stupid fears about hospitals, " where they cut you up," as the saying is.

But, for all they are ignorant and primitive and, one might almost say, half-savage, there are, I can see, many good qualities in the Kishtwaris. They are good, honest, truthful country-folk, living decent lives, with an honest pride in their class and labour. One great thing is that there is no trace here of the Platonic love which is so marked and unpleasant a feature of the social life of the Dard tribes, from Gurais on the Gilgit Road to Nagar and Chitral, among whom even the dancing-girls are dancing-boys. One wonders by the way whether this perverse inclination in the Indus valley and the neighbouring glens is a tradition transmitted from the invasion by Alexander's Greeks and from his Diadochi. It is certain at least that in Persia, which before the Greek invasion was innocent of the vice, this Platonism has ever since been mortally prevalent in all classes. Even if we reject as unproven the observation which would trace among the Kafirs of the Hindu-Kush the very blood and features of the Macedonian soldiery, it is likely enough that the Dards—like the Kashmiris—were in some way or other, perhaps by consanguinity, at least by culture, influenced by the vicinity of Hellenism. But in the Kishtwaris, as they now are, there is no sign of any kind of Grecian derivation. They are plain, honest Indians of the hill-type, dearly clinging to the style of Rajput, poor, hard-working, not luxurious.

A quality in them, which at once impresses the stranger, is that, poor and dirty and ignorant as they are, they yet bear unmistakeably the stamp of the gentleman. They are now, I fancy, much as were the Scottish Highlanders—the clansmen, that is, not the educated Chiefs and Duniewassals—before the 'forty-five. They are perfectly frank and manly and independent, yet they are invariably courteous with a sort of innate fact and breeding. It is as though they knew their own worth and yet were ready to recognize superiors and degrees in rank and power in a world where, all being men, yet no two men are ever equal but some must be born to command and others to obey. They show nothing either of foolish flattery or uneasy assumption. They address me quietly as "huzur"—the "presence"—naturally and without effort or a forced politeness; but, quite as easily and naturally, without assumption or offence they state their obvious superiority to me, for instance, in hill-climbing and agility. They take for granted, in a word, that as between men of decent conduct facts will always be faced frankly and without pretence. Throughout India this instinctive and innate courtesy, the habit of the gentleman, abides in all who bear the name of Rajput or even claim a cognate history and training. You may find the Rajput occasionally, sapped by untrammelled power and luxury, in the mischievous environment of an intriguing harem, vicious, effeminate and profligate ; but I have never known one who was ill-mannered or could be mistaken for, after all, anything but a gentleman. Even among the Kolis of Gujarat, those who were their soldiery and are often near enough connected, the Baria Kolis of the Panch Mahals for instance, bear the stamp and dignity of a peasant *noblesse.* I have known such Kolis well, in wild famine days in my younger life, and, with one exception in a man from a city suburb and him drunken, I have never seen behaviour which, even if a little rude and rural, was not that of a natural gentleman. It is curious and in these proclaimed days of democracy has in it something of a *nota bene,* that there are certain places and peoples, under favouring conditions, where the breath and flavour of nobility emanates from the poorest and most ignorant. The Highlanders of Scotland furnish to this day an obvious instance and it is still true to say that the impoverished crofter on the western shores of Ross is in his easy manner and his simple courtesy a gentleman, unmistakeable. The Hungarian peasantry of the

Alföld supplies another illustration. Of these, of course, many have even technically the right to rank *inter nobiles et illustres,* though an unfortunate apeing of German Court etiquette in the aristocracy has slurred and warped the national and genuine distinction. But these peasants do not derive their manners from the technical nobility of a few. They owe it to their heredity and environment as free, fighting men on a free soil. The Hungarian peasant has his faults; he has a weakness for an unnecessary swagger, for *la panache*; like most men of Hungarian blood—even when bred in a colder climate—he is passionate to excess, not only in his loves, but also in his raging anger; but with these faults, and with his virtues of loyalty and generosity, he is a gentleman without any doubt. See him for a moment beside a German of any rank or a Slav outside of the highest class, and the distinction leaps to the eye.

Is it a fighting history which bestows this fine noblity of manner? or is it a tradition of freedom and of power? Are there some peoples, like the Teutonic races, to whom it is denied by birth? It seems clear at any rate that it is incompatible with certain qualities and pursuits, with everything for instance that Aristotle stigmatized as mean trades. But between him who has it and him who has it not, the clearest difference and most absolute touchstone is surely that uneasy claim to "rights" which is the last disqualification of certain social classes. In modern Europe, for instance, the lower middle-classes and the industrial artisans are at every turn to be found "standing up for their rights ", and there is not a moment when they are not busy suspecting some one or other of interfering with those precious rights of theirs. And it is precisely these classes in Europe who have sunk to the lowest depths in all that concerns the social amenities and behaviour. In India, again, there are regions of a more democratic tinge where it would unhappily be impossible to apply to the inhabitants the adjectives which, with every title and justification, I have used of the Rajput and even of the Koli, as there are classes to whom, as to similar trading classes in Europe, the peasant of Kishtwar might have many a lesson to teach. Uneasy—pushing—uncertain of himself—of his position —of his rights—loud for his rights—clamorous for his rights—and uneasy—damnably uneasy—well, these are not the qualities of the Kishtwari, the Highlander or the gentleman.

CHAPTER IX.

AFTER GURAL AGAIN—THEIR APPEARANCE—A MISS—LOOKING FOR TAHR—A DIFFICULT CLIMB.

FRIDAY, the 13th, the Mussulman Sabbath, dawned a perfect day at last, and it was with joy that the servants and I saw the beautiful sun again after three long days of rain. It was joy merely to look upon the hills, clear-cut and distinct, and looking, after all this rain, as if quite close to the eye ; to see the Gujjars' buffaloes grazing on the hill-side ; and to hear the bees buzzing from flower to flower. I strolled about with my dog a little before breakfast, for the mere joy of tasting the sunny morning air, and the dog raced up-hill and down-hill, barking for very lightness of heart and flinging himself through the bracken after the cowering chikor.

In the afternoon at three, I left for the eastern slopes of the hill with my *shikari* and a local man to look for two *gural* which had been marked there in the early morning. By a zig-zag track, where the cattle of this upland are driven to graze, we went down the slope till, by a turn to the north, we found ourselves under the cover of a single deodar, jutting out from a projecting cliff. Here at about 300 yards I faced the rocks and bushes where the *gural* had last been seen. There was a concave curve between our tree and those rocks and above the curve hung the crags which had been the lair of the panther that I had killed. We spent no little time in searching, with the aid of prismatic glasses, before the *gural* could be spotted, and in the end it was the hill-man who saw them first with the naked eye. They were two, one well in shade under the overhanging ledge of a reddish rock, the other on a single stone against a background of bush in the sunlight. Once they were marked, I was able to watch them carefully through the glasses, and it was only then and later on when I watched their movements that I really grasped what the *gural* is and what he looks like. I was enabled to watch these two for a long time, for we had seen them by four o'clock and we sat in the same place without moving till a quarter to seven.

The *gural* is in kind a capricorn, but much smaller than his cousin, the *serow,* his height being that of a small sheep. In many ways he resembles the Indian *chinkara* or gazelle, especially in his manner of scratching his head with his hind leg. But he does not stand as high as the *chinkara* and the chest and fore-part of the body is relatively much deeper and sturdier. He has not the graceful elegance of the *chinkara,* but he has an added strength and force. The horns are much shorter than those of the Indian gazelle, the greatest length only eight inches and a good head being anything of six inches or upwards. The horns curve backwards in a single curve without that upward retorsion of the tip which is so light and graceful in the *chinkara.* Nor has the *gural* got the restlessness and that unceasing twitch of the tail which is the habit of the Indian animal. The skin, too, is grey rather than brown and there is a well-defined line, almost black in colour, along the spine. The position of the one on the stone in the sunlight was exactly that of the chamois as I had often seen it in pictures, the head bent well to the side, the four feet bunched very close together. What was most astonishing was the absence of all movement. It is, of course, this immobility, taken along with the protective colouring, which makes it so difficult to detect a *gural* or to hit him when he is seen.

For at least half an hour after our coming, the two animals remained standing perfectly still where they were. Then suddenly they jumped from their rock, moved on a few yards through the bushes, and again came to a stand, being now entirely hidden from our sight by the undergrowth. It took nearly another hour before they again moved and began to browze. Even then they persisted in clinging to the few yards of bush and undergrowth where a shot was an impossibility, though I prayed and hoped that they might leave the little nallah where they were and come out on the grassy slope, where I could have got an easy shot at a reasonable distance. It was their smallness which I had never realized properly before. Now, seen against a rose-bush, they hardly reached even the lowest twigs. Seeing this I felt that, after all, I had no particular reason to be ashamed of my shooting on Monday, for to hit so small an animal on the move in a bad light was more difficult than I had guessed. At last after waiting till after half-past six, without seeing any sign of the animals coming our way and with every indication of their continuing to browze in the same place, I held a whispered consultation with my *shikari*. At the same moment a third *gural* appeared silhouetted clearly against the sky-line on a rock. But the distance was more than three hundred yards, which in my opinion put the shot out of the question. This animal stood there a few seconds and then disappeared down-hill.

After much debate, my *shikari* and I decided that the only thing left to do was to try and stalk the two animals which we had watched from the beginning. The danger was in the first fifty yards. This space lay within the field of vision of the *gural* and, if they noticed us here, they would be sure to break away. If, however, we could cross this space unobserved—but it was bad going over limestone—we should be under cover from the curve of the hill till we got close to our animals. It was a poor chance but it had to be risked. We left the hill-man behind to signal to us, when we got near, if the *gural* had moved and, very gingerly, we started on our stalk. But, sure enough, when we had accomplished it with infinite precautions, the *gural* had disappeared, and we saw the hill-man's hand waving to signify they had gone down the hill. This was disappointing but hardly unexpected. My *shikari* then prospected further and came back to say he had found a solitary *gural* further on. We then crawled down a grass-slope till we reached a point where, dead below us, a *gural* stood with his neck stretched out to the side, peering from a projecting rock into the ravine underneath. The place, however, was very awkward for a shot. I tried one position to find a bush in the way; then I pushed myself up again backwards on the very edge of the cliff. Again a piece of bush got in the way. I found myself forced at last to lean over the edge very uncomfortably and to take the shot, lying on my back with my rifle pointing between my feet. I did, however, take the shot, perhaps hastily, in this position and I missed. The lie of the country gave no chance for a second barrel. The stalk had ended in a failure.

There was, however, much to console me for the failure. First of all, I had had a splendid view of these animals as they live, which was worth a good deal. Moreover, when I got back to the top of the hill, I was met by a superb prospect to the south-east over the snow-covered range of Pangi, lying between us on Pahlma and the famous Kulu valley. The highest part of the range was of the shape of a wedge, covered with snow; and the whitened summits of the whole mountain chain were flushed and suffused with the delicate pink lights of the setting sun. A cool evening breeze blew directly on us. Not a cloud was to be seen and the landscape at that passing hour was at once peaceful and magnificent. It was the quiet *nunc dimittis* of a perfect summer day, among the stone-hewn, stone-fretted masses of the Asian mountains.

The next day, the 14th of July, was equally fine and the camp was again cheery and happy. The post-coolie arrived bringing letters from my wife and also letters from my mother at home and the English papers which had been saved by a fortunate chance from the floating mail-bags of the Mongolia. Moreover, I had now good hopes of the recovery of at least one of the two *gural* I had wounded. One of the Gujjars camped beside me had seen kites and vultures hovering in that direction the previous night and he was now going to look at the place with every hope of finding the body and saving the skull and horns. This was cheering news and I settled down to my mail with a light heart, after deciding to go out in the afternoon after a *tahr* which had been marked on the farther side of our hill.

We left the camp, accordingly, a little after three, going again to the eastern slope of the hill. From that point we had first a small climb to the top and had then to descend on the other side. The top of the hill was here covered with wild rhubarb, of which I had been eating for the last few days and of which we gathered more on our return. In the meantime we went further and further down, first through forest and then down fissures in the bare limestone crags. The descent was difficult in the extreme, as the angle was nearly perpendicular. The foot-hold had to be eked out the whole way by a firm grip of the fingers on branches or corners of rock, and every now and then we had to slide carefully or to leap from one projecting point of stone to another. Not a step could be taken without first looking and making sure where the foot was to be placed. The mere exertion of moving was considerable, while the effort to preserve utter silence, the care needed to prevent the iron-shod stick in my hand from striking a stone, and the frequent dashes after a loosened pebble to keep it from rolling noisily downhill, all added heavily to the labour of the descent. When we had reached the bottom of that part of the slope which was still grassy and wooded, I sat down for a few minutes' rest, while the *shikari* looked over the adjoining nallah to see if the goat was still there. He returned in a few minutes to say he had seen the animal, but a goodish way down and on the move. Thus there was nothing for it but to face the further descent among the rocks, to me at least, with their precipitous prospects, an unpleasant obstacle. But we went down and further down, till at last an actual vertical precipice hindered all further progress. Here, then, we lay on a rock hanging over the precipice and looked over cautiously for the *tahr*. But we could not find him anywhere and it was only too painfully clear that the animal must have moved on even lower.

The two hill-men who had accompanied me now volunteered to try what seemed to be our only possible chance, to cross the nallah, that is, scale the precipice on the other side, and come round and back lower down. In this way there was some faint hope that the *tahr* might be turned back towards us in the nallah. Before I consented, however, I assured myself by repeated questions that the men were really willing to do this and that they had no fears of slipping and falling on the wall of rock. I let them go only after they had told me time after time that they were anxious to try it and were not afraid. Their only precaution, indeed, was to remove their coats and their grass-shoes. After they had gone, I had leisure to look round and see exactly where I had got to. To my great surprise I saw, just opposite me, the projecting spur and trees where I had spent the midday hours of the previous Monday. Now I recognized that the nallah on whose ledge I was lying was at the edge of the very wall of rock down which I had seen the herd of *tahr* climb as I watched the hill on that day. We had come down, I now found, between the deodars on the upper ledges and over the less precipitous of the upper crags to a point just above the abrupt and vertical face of rock. I remembered also that on that day I had asked about this particular place and whether the hill-men could traverse it; and when they said, 'yes, with some difficulty,' I had laughed and said that I at least was not going to try to rival them. Yet here after all I had come, in the excitement of the chase and with the idea that the *tahr* was just in front of me and might still be overtaken. As the hill-men began to turn downwards, I braced myself up against the side of the rock, with my *shikari* holding my leg to support me against the recoil when I fired, and waited for the shot. But all the labour and all the waiting was useless. The animal had gone too far, and the hill-men came back to shout that the *tahr* had moved off further down to the right across ground that was quite impassable and that nothing more could be done.

The climb back was exhausting in the extreme. We had to haul ourselves up as if climbing a rope in a gymnasium, our feet clinging to points of stone or fissures while the weight of the body was pulled up with such grip as could be got on the edges of the rock or on bushes. We stopped every thirty or forty foot,

I should think, out of breath and with tired muscles. Mercifully we were in shade the whole time and the air was cool. But when at last I reached the top, every muscle in thigh and leg and not a few in back and arm and shoulders ached as if they had been stretched on the rack. We sat down on the top for a good rest and I passed my cigarettes round to my *shikari* and our two Kishtwari companions. The view was again superb over Pangi and the air delightful ; and the weariness passed quickly in the bracing atmosphere of the summit.

When we returned, I met the Gujjar with the head of the missing *gural* with decent horns, 7 inches long. This was a real pleasure, less only than the joys of a good hot bath, of dinner, and of bed. One of the delights of these hills is the pure water that wells out from innumerable springs and I drank much and freely when I got home. There is no need in the mountains for those precautions which are imposed on one, distastefully enough, by the insanitary conditions of the Kashmir valley or in India. Water from a hill spring can be drunk unboiled, unfiltered and without touch of chlorine or chlorogen. The milk I get is milked straight from the cow by the Gujjar women beside my camp and the cows graze night and day on the open hill. I have rich cream each morning with my breakfast porridge and the milk I drink is not boiled or heated. One needs to have lived in India and to have known the daily recurring disgust of using water and milk that have become insipid, if not smoky and nauseating, through boiling, to appreciate the simple pleasure of drinking them fresh and good.

CHAPTER X.

FEVER—A BEAT FOR BEAR—ANOTHER PANTHER KILLED —I TRY FOR A THIRD PANTHER—SUNSHINE AND RAIN.

On the 15th, when I woke, the air was again raw and damp, and mists hung thickly over trees and tents. As I still felt tired, I got up slowly and sat down under a tree to write letters after a leisurely breakfast. One of the letters I wrote was to our doctor in our late Indian headquarters, to say how much the better I was for my leave and tell him how I had got rid of the ailments with which I had worried him while we were together in our station. But after I had sent off my post and had luncheon, I lay down, as I still felt tired, and found myself presently shaking and shivering with a fit of ague. However, the sun came out and the ague was not particularly severe. A beat for bear had already been arranged for the afternoon and I was reluctant to upset the arrangements. In spite, therefore, of feeling every symptom of fever, I determined to get up and go out at five o'clock, fortified in this by the fact that the thermometer showed my temperature to be still moderate. The place where I was to sit in the beat was luckily at no great distance and I struggled there in good time, though I felt shaky and wretched. But the beat was a miserable failure after all, badly managed, and it had hardly begun before the bear broke out to the side. I could follow what was happening from the shouts and the movements of the beaters, but was too far off to catch even a glimpse of the animal. All things considered, I was heartily glad when it was over and I was free to find my way back, very slowly and painfully, to my tent and my bed. By this time, I was really feeling thoroughly bad, though the temperature was again climbing downwards by the time I returned. The camp was to have moved next morning but in the circumstances I hardly felt equal to a long walk up a steep ascent within so short a time and had to countermand the orders, resigning myself, as I thought, to wasting another day where we were.

Next day, in spite of the usual quinine deafness, I felt distinctly better. I therefore gave orders to build a *machan* or shelter in a tree against that evening, when I should tie up for a panther. This brute had for weeks been making itself a nuisance to the Gujjars by carrying off their sheep and for the last three days had been annoying me by prowling round my tent, so that I had to tie my dog at sunset to the foot of my bed to keep him safe. The Gujjars had been asking me for the last few days to try to shoot the panther and one of them brought me a young dog from the settlement to use as a bait for the purpose. My *shikari* and I accordingly went out in the evening accompanied by the Gujjar and his dog, and I found that the *shikari* had made a very good *machan* on the lower branches of a deodar, beside a small bare patch of grass, where the dog was to be tied. The dog was tied up accordingly, and we climbed into our tree, the Gujjar, instead of going back, insisting on remaining beside us and finding himself a perch on an upper branch. The proceedings now took their usual Indian course : the dog howled ; the panther first coughed on my right and then crept out stealthily on my left ; I let him come up quietly through the bushes till he was about twelve paces away, and put one bullet through his head and the second into his convulsed body, just to make sure. He was quite a fine animal, measuring seven foot two inches between sticks when killed, with his colour darker than is usual in Kashmir and more like the usual Indian leopard. The poor dog was, as can be fancied, overjoyed to be unchained and, after leaping up on his master, ran off at full speed to tell his adventures to his canine friends in the Gujjar encampment. By far the most amusing part of the show was the enthusiasm of the Gujjars. The leopard is not so common a visitor in these parts as in the forest villages of India, and is much more dreaded, while the Gujjars' subsistence depends upon the herds of which this sly and audacious thief takes toll. It is, therefore, hardly surprising that they greet a leopard's downfall with exaggerated delight. As we approached our camp, carrying the dead body, the man who had been with us ran ahead shouting and prancing. He yelled the glad tidings downhill to the little settlement. And up they came at once, all who were then at home, four women with six or seven children, all ablaze with excitement, to chortle with glee and gloat over the body of their *dushman*, their enemy, as they emphatically called him. They turned him over, and pulled his tail and counted his teeth, and mocked him and jested and abused, and it took a long time before I finally got them quiet and saw them go down again to their homes, chattering and laughing as they went.

So far I had heard of these two panthers only and I had now disposed of them both. But, after I had gone to bed that night, a third panther actually did turn up. At first I could hardly believe my ears, when I heard four or five growls quite close to my tent and found my dog moving uneasily and growling in a half-frightened way in response. But immediately after, my servant came running up to confirm the fact and ask me to tie up the dog, and the *shikari* followed to say he had also heard the beast moving round the camp. Could this, I wondered, be the female of the animal I had killed that afternoon ? This could apparently be the only explanation. If so, she was probably just behind her fellow, when he was shot, and must have followed us and hung round the camp on account of the dead body. By the note of the growls, too, it was evident that she was in an angry mood. It seemed to me that there was fear that she might carry off my dog and I had a good log-fire lit in front of my tent.

The next day, the 17th, was again cloudy and showery. I felt much better, however, and got up after quinine and breakfast. The post came again, always a pleasure, with letters from my wife and papers and an official communication which gave me satisfaction.

There was melancholy, however, in the news of poor Sir Herbert Beerbohm Tree's death—a great personality and my friend's step-brother.

The day continued to be so unpleasant, wet and misty, that serious *shikar* was out of the question. It was not even any use my *shikari* attempting to go out and mark down any game beforehand, a step which should always be taken when possible. In the afternoon, however, wrapped in a waterproof, I went to the western slopes, where I had not yet been, on the chance of finding *gural.* Moreover, the third panther had been seen by a Gujjar moving in that direction in the morning and there was just a bare possibility that a tie-up on that side might prove successful. At any rate I arranged for a *machan* to be ready there as well. The search for *gural* was at first distinctly hopeful, for, when we got to a bare little precipice of rock in the middle of the pine-forest, a solitary *gural* could be seen grazing on the top. We lay down under cover to watch his movements ; for the chances were that he would come slowly down towards us, the water from which the *gural* usually drink being close by. After we had lain there for five minutes, however, to our horror the figure of a Gujjar woman appeared from the forest near the *gural,* cutting grass. Naturally the *gural* saw her as soon as we did, snorted in alarm, and rushed back into the upper forest. So that chance at least was gone. From the sporting point of view those Gujjars are certainly an unmitigated nuisance. Their herds drive the shyer wild animals—the goats, the chamois, and the red bear—further and further away into the highest altitudes.

And near their encampments, when by chance game does remain, it is constantly being scared at the least suitable moments by their women and children fetching wood or cutting grass and whistling and singing. In this particular case, the little encampment had been warned beforehand that I was going that way that day and its dwellers requested not to go into that part of the forest, and they had gladly, and I fully believe sincerely, promised not to do so. But intelligence is not the Gujjar's strong point, and I put down this unfortunate woman's ill-timed intrusion to sheer stupidity. At any rate, after her appearance, the search for *gural* had to be given up and we came back a little way to our *machan*. The dog we used was the same that we had had the previous day; and the slaughter of his enemy under his nose and his subsequent reward of a platter full of milk and bread had apparently quickly taught him to look on the whole thing as a game. When tied up and left alone, he gave a few slight whimpers; but almost immediately set to playing with the peg to which he was tied, to jumping at insects, and to digging; and finally, after a good curl or two, he soundly fell to sleeping. This was satisfactory to himself and from an impersonal point of view I should not have grudged him the simple pleasure; but, as a bait for a hungry carnivore, it made him less than useless. After waiting nearly two hours, I gave it up in disgust and we returned to our tents with our contented dog, to be met by the news that another Gujjar had in the afternoon seen the panther near their settlement on the eastern side but had not had the sense to let us know. And still it rained.

It was still raining on the 18th when I rose and to move camp was again impossible. By this time I was sick unto death of the drip-drip-drip of the water and the gloom of mist and cloud and the cold monotony of this dampness. I love the sun and his glorious radiance, and feel that, in an earlier age and other conditions, I must, like a Magian, have been a worshipper of his chariot. Rain, at the best of times, I hate, nor have I ever been able to understand what induced the Sanskrit poets and their later Indian imitators to place the flowering of love in the melancholy season of the rains. In those days when Krishna, whose body is dark like the thundercloud and who under the name of Meghraj is the ruler of the mists, lets flow the waters of the sky and drenches the sopping earth with their floods, I could, indeed, understand a wistful sorrow in separation; but, for the blossoming of new love and the torture of passion, why, even the flame and fiery spirit would be drowned in the vast vat of insipid fluid. For me, I would be like the dial, if I could, and remain steadfast to a *horas non imputo nisi serenas*. When I retired from service, I should seek my residence in the dry oases of Arabia, could I only be certain of transporting there on some magic carpet the comforts of a good club and the hostelries and theatres of London and of Paris. One is told, it is true, of the terrors of the vertical sun in the Indian summer; and I still remember how an older friend warned me in my novitiate never, in that climate and country, to lay aside the fear of two things, the serpent and the sun. Nor can I in fact nor dare I deny the sun's fierce implacability and his deadly sting in his summer might. Yet after all, in India more than elsewhere, it is the sun which keeps the bodies of men clean and healthful and our souls fresh and alert. His desiccating rays cleanse the city with its dirty slums and dispel the lurking pestilence ; they purify the cess-pools of the town and the polluted river bed. Even the cool shade of the banian-tree, by the road-side, near the large well where the water plashes pleasantly as the leathern bag is drawn slowly to the surface, is the gift, after all, of the sun. But best of all, loveable surely at all times and to all men, is the tempered warmth of the Mediterranean sunshine in a garden above the blue of the tideless sea.

No sun, however, came to cheer us this day, though the clouds gradually lifted in the afternoon and the sky gave some promise of clearing up. I went out again at three in the afternoon to the same western slope to look for the *gural,* after giving orders for another *machan* to be built on the east, near the spot where I had killed the leopard two days before. Our walk after *gural* took us by a steep climb to the western summit, the highest peak of the whole hill ; and the clouds had by this time so far lifted that I could enjoy a splendid view over that side of the province. Below us lay Moghul Maidan, which, as I had told the local people and they remembered, must, after God had created Kishtwar, have been pushed to its present depression by a surreptitious poke from Satan's finger. There, too, was the confluence of the water rushing down the Wardwan valley into the stream from the Sinthan pass. Opposite across the valley and lower than we were, was Yandribal, formerly a famous shooting-centre, with its grim bare crags where the goats live. Further west, past Yandribal, a four days' journey up was the mountain above Pambar, half-covered in mist and sprinkled with snow. There I might still go, if I had the time. For, while at Tsingam, I had received information of two large ibex on that mountain and I had sent to have the news verified. Should it turn out correct, and should I still have time after the loss of so many days on account of rain, I had the intention of crossing the Wardwan valley and finding my way to the ibex ground above Pambar, returning from there to Kashmir by a little-known pass to the north of Sinthan. Nearer to us, but to the north of Pambar, I could see also the high grass-covered summit of Lowmarg, a well-known shooting-ground but difficult to climb. After the rain, the atmosphere was wonderfully clear and it was easy to see with the naked eye the cattle that were ploughing on the lower slopes of the hills across the valley. From where we stood, so steep up and down are these mountains, it looked as if the river were straight beneath us and a plumbed line from our hands might fathom its waters. The aspect on this western slope of the hill is indeed lovely, finer by far than the eastern side, with more profuse vegetation, thicker and loftier trees, and gorgeous masses of wild-flowers.

But though we climbed up to the crags that surmount the precipitous reverse side of the mountain, we could catch no sight of *gural*. So we returned soon after five to our tents for a cup of tea before going to sit up for the panther. I had managed to borrow a new dog this evening and set out with him to find an excellent *machan* built beside a fairly large patch of open ground. At the very moment I reached there, I was cheered by the sound of a leopard's loud growl, not, it seemed, in the best of tempers and probably hungry. As the sound came a little to the east and beyond us, it was likely that his evening prowl would bring him close to our tree. I feared, however, that the experience of two nights ago might have scared him (or should I not rather say 'her ?') and that she (I will say 'she,' for I am sure this was a female) would not approach the bait too closely. But into the tree we climbed and the dog howled bravely. At first there was no further sign from the panther. Then, some fifteen minutes later, a tumultuous outcry from a little parliament of crows on my right, cries and squeaks of contempt and hatred, let me infer that the panther, the best hated of all jungle animals, was passing beneath the rookery ; and, after another five minutes, I saw a suspicious movement of some bushes to my left, caused certainly by no wind. I now felt certain that the panther was there, and I watched the ground carefully to protect the poor dog from any sudden spring. But would she venture ? I still felt doubtful. I recalled the events of two nights ago and the more I thought, the more convinced I was that the female must have been directly behind her mate, had seen him killed, and had watched us getting down from the tree and carrying the body home. Thus only could I account for the way she had prowled round our camp, immediately after. And, if I was right, could I suppose she would again venture near a *machan?* I could hardly believe she would. The next fifteen or twenty minutes would, however, decide the question. If she were hungry enough, if she had the nerve like so many Indian leopards that live in the outskirts of villages and are used to the coming and going of men, then, after a little circumspection, she would assuredly come with all the audacity of a bullying brigand to the appetizing meal before her nose. But if the twist of appetite was not so sharp or if, wild inhabitant of the remoter forests that she was, she feared her unfamiliar enemy, man, too much, then as certainly she would lie under cover till darkness gave her the chance of a hurried snatch at her prey. Fifteen minutes passed and twenty and half-an-hour. Then I whispered to my *shikari* to ask him whether he would like to stay on longer, as I felt it was useless. He still had hopes, he answered, and I agreed to wait longer. The Kashmiris have an amount of respect and fear for the leopard which is not a little exaggerated and have a corresponding admiration for the slaughter of one of those dreaded animals. I felt, therefore, that it was unfair to deprive the *shikari* of what after all was still a slight chance, though my own experience of such shooting led me to consider further waiting useless. After all, I admitted, there was still the possibility that at twilight the beast's hunger might overcome her discretion and impel her to a quick rush during which, if I were lucky, I might knock her over. I waited, therefore, with the clouds lifting and the sky becoming brighter, and a cold wind setting in from the east, which made my hands and feet feel numb and my body chilled and starved. The sun at last set and the shadows of the twilight closed upon us. But the panther would not come out of her cover. At last with two loud and angry growls (or rather bellows) close beside me but again on my right hand, she announced that she was furious with us and had definitely decided not to try for the dog. There was nothing for it now but to give up our hopes. I shouted for the owner of the dog and got out of the tree, stiff and half-frozen. To wait longer was useless, for there was no moon and in the darkness the dog might be killed six times over without my being able to shoot the leopard. As we walked home, I kept my rifle loaded and ready and had the dog held on the leash. For I felt sure that the panther would be our silent escort through the wood and I had once before in India, while returning from a similar tie-up in the darkness, had a leopard jump out of a bush and carry away a dog from under my very eyes. This time, however, our leopard made no such attempt and we returned home unmolested.

CHAPTER XI.

A NEW CAMP—A TAHR KILLED—A DIFFICULT DESCENT—ANOTHER GURAL.

THE 19th of July was at last a beautiful sunny day and we set to work at once to move camp. Coolies came and head-loads were made up; and, after breakfast, we set out on our climb to the eastern summit. Our march was a small one, rather under two hours, to our new encampment. This was situated on a narrow ridge running between and joining the mountain on which we had so far been living to the next rather higher peak of the same range. The two mountains are almost parallel with this ridge at right angles, or rather at a slightly obtuse angle, to either, so that the inner sides of the two mountains and the connecting ridge form a sort of circus, very precipitous, very stony, and almost bare of trees. On the ridge itself the spot on which we pitched was magnificent. It was approached over the softest turf through a forest of splendid lofty deodars. Far below on the one side rushed the Chandra Bagha river, whose roar reached us up here always and in a favouring wind very loudly, though its level is three thousand foot lower. The view extended on the other side over the Wardwan valley to Lowmarg and further to the left to the snow-capped mountain

Photograph by Vishinath of Shrinagar.

A GORGE ON THE CHANDRA-BAGHA.

range that lies between Kishtwar and Kashmir. But the supreme glory was the multitude of flowers. Forget-me-nots predominated, so that the small patch of meadow where I lay showed in the main, upon its green ground, an effect of pervading bright, almost metallic, blue, like Limoges enamel. There were great masses of buttercups too, scattered among and diversifying the prevailing colour, and, through it all, powdered in whites and creams and light pale purples were other flowers whose names I did not know. Bees in untold numbers buzzed and flew and settled, and bright speckled reddish-brown butterflies whirled and played in a constant round with one another.

My dog, on the last upper slopes and on this little meadow between the rocks, was as if mad with joy. He flung pine-cones to himself into the air to catch again, and rushed round and round and down into the forest and back again to the meadow as if possessed. Only one drawback we found to our little paradise, the want of water. There was, indeed, what passed for a spring, but it was now, after the trampling of many cattle, nothing but a dirty muddy puddle, so filthy that its water could not be used even for washing. We had, therefore, at once to send back every vessel we possessed to be filled at the lower spring near the last of the Gujjar encampments.

In the afternoon, shortly after four, accompanied by my *shikari* and the two local men who had been with us all the time, I left the camp to look for *tahr*, the wild goats of these mountains. We made our way cautiously among the topmost crags, and the *shikari* went to one cliff with one of the men, while the other, Laldin, crept a little further to another projection ; and I waited under a tree between the two. A very few minutes had passed when I saw Laldin gently beckoning to me, with the Indian signal of the outstretched downward-pointing hand pulled inwards, that I should come and join him where he sat. I found my way slowly to him and he whispered that he had marked a *tahr* down below. Now we crept a little further down on the steep slope till, turning flat on my breast, I crouched beside him on the last projection and looked over gently and cautiously. It took me some minutes before I could make out the goat and my *shikari* had time to steal over quietly from his rock and lie beside us. Then, with the glasses, he found the animal and marked his horns and told me more accurately where to look. At last I saw him too, a small reddish patch, hardly perceptible, moving slowly, grazing, through the high grass and bushes. Slowly I got my rifle to the shoulder, while I wormed head and shoulders over the edge of 'the cliff, with Laldin firmly gripping my outstretched legs. The *tahr* stood still for a moment with the upper part of his body showing above the grass, a little over 250 yards away and almost straight below me. As steadily as I could, I got my sights on him and pressed the trigger. He stumbled, but recovered himself and moved on, but I took a second shot just before he turned the corner of the nallah, and had the satisfaction of seeing him stumble again. Both shots had hit, and with my 400-450 cordite rifle they should, I thought, be mortal. Laldin got up at once and rushed as quickly as the rocks allowed to the next point of the hill to watch the wounded animal. In a few seconds he appeared again to signal to the *shikari*, in that wonderful and ample language of gestures which those men employ, that the animal was dead, but that another *tahr* was in sight and I should come to the place.

For me the way over was very difficult, as I clung to every roughness and fissure in the rocks with my fingers; and it was not quickly that I reached the other side. By the time I got there, the second *tahr* had made off and there was nothing to do but wait till Laldin and the other hill-men reached the dead animal. A welcome shout soon told us they had found him and we climbed slowly back over the rocks to our camp, leaving the men to skin the animal and bring back the trophies. Some of the camp-coolies, when they heard the news, also faced the cliffs to bring back a share of meat for themselves ; but the greater number, I found, though they started, thought better of it when they saw the climb they would have to do and slunk back quietly to the camp-fire. The horns were of moderate size only, 10 inches, but that was the first of the goats I had ever shot and I was quite satisfied. This certainly is a trophy whose value lies in its rarity, for the *tahr* is found only in a very few tracts in all the Himalayas and his shooting as a rule entails a deal of difficulty and endurance. The men who have shot these goats are few and the beautiful horns of the ibex are more often seen than the smaller trophy of his lesser cousin. Every one in the camp shared my satisfaction ; and the tough, rather rank-smelling meat. was divided greedily by the camp-followers, one quarter being religiously reserved as an offering to the shrine on the hill-side.

At night there was a small shower and I woke up on the 20th to find the hill-side again heavily shrouded in damp dripping mist. My *shikari* did go out in the morning to see if he could mark down any more goats, hoping that perhaps the mist might rise ; but the hope was unfulfilled and he returned at breakfast-time without having been able to see more than a dozen yards before his nose. The day was growing warmer, however, and there seemed every likelihood that in time the mist would lift, and we decided to go down the hill at noon and wait for the afternoon movements of the animals on their way to graze. A walk along a path through the upper rocks for about a mile took us to the starting-point of our descent, a grass-slope but at an angle which was all but straight. Every step had here to be taken with caution, and it was necessary to hold on firmly to grass and bush the whole way. My *shikari* went in front, going backwards most of the way, partly for his own ease, but mainly in order to give me help when required. I accomplished a large part of the descent sliding and thanked my stars that my clothes were made of the stoutest Kashmiri *puttoo* cloth. Behind me followed two coolies, the one, Laldin, a hill-man of Kishtwar, who laughed at these difficulties ; the other a Kashmiri, to whom the slope was almost as insurmountable and alarming as to me. The grass was rank and high, and the stones and sudden holes which it covered could not be seen, till a slip or fall, broken by the grip of hand on bush, made them only too painfully known. When, three or four hundred feet lower down, we reached a solitary and dejected pine tree, we turned to the north and descended the slope diagonally at a milder angle to our left. But the slope itself was not much less steep than the ravine down which we had to climb straight, and I found it nearly as difficult to keep my footing while crossing as I had on the vertical descent. By the time we reached the rock where we were to wait for the afternoon hours, I was as exhausted as by unusual exertions in a gymnasium, and, though the distance had in reality been small, I found we had been nearly two hours on our way. By this time the mist had cleared up and the rock on which we sat was fully exposed to the sun and the heat tormenting; and for two hours there was nothing to do except sit stock-still in utter silence.

At four, my *shikari* noticed a *gural* move below us. I crept along beside him and lay flat on the rock to observe the animal. It was about 200 yards away from us, half-hidden in grass and looking very small; but, through the glasses, we could see that the horns were good. Was I to shoot or not? I wanted another *tahr* really and the shot might scare the goats away. On the other hand it seemed a pity not to take what was given: and, if I did not fire at the *gural*, it might after all easily happen that I should get no chance at *tahr* either. I decided to try for the *gural*. To get into place for the shot was not easy, and I took most of the skin of my left hand off on the rough surface of the rock as I lowered myself over the edge into a suitable position.

Then I fired, and the shot, I believe, went low; the *gural* jumped but gave me another chance; and again I missed by an inch or two. A third shot was also a trifle low; and then, for a moment, the *gural* stood silhouetted against a rock and I took a steadier fourth shot.

This time the bullet again struck the rock, but the animal stumbled badly before he jumped into the *nallah* and disappeared under cover of thick bush. I was uncertain whether I had hit or not, and the *shikari*, from the sound of the bullet on the rock, was sure I had missed again. But when we had waited another ten minutes and there was no further movement, we decided to send Laldin and the other coolie down round and below the *nallah* in the hope of pushing the animal up towards me. They went below and had got to the mouth of the *nallah*, when the *gural* suddenly rose and rushed past Laldin only three or four yards away, going stiffly, but so close to the men that I dared not fire. The *gural* went up a few yards and then turned again to some rose bushes and lay down beneath them. The men came slowly up the *nallah* and, just beside the rock where my last shot had hit, found a profusion of blood and further drops of blood along the track that the *gural* had taken in bolting. They came up to us and reported accordingly. What had happened was now clear. The bullet had gone clean through the body and had evidently pierced the stomach and the animal was now dying. The only question to decide was whether I should face the steep climb downwards to the rose bushes and try to get another shot at once; or whether, knowing that his death must come quickly, I should leave him and wait where I was, on the chance of *tahr* appearing. Myself I was afraid the animal might make for water and get lost, and also wanted to put him out of pain quickly; but the men were certain he would never rise again, so great had been the loss of blood, and were most anxious that I should wait for possible *tahr*. And in the end, helped to that decision perhaps by a natural disinclination to face the further descent when I was already tired, I agreed to their views and stayed where I was. The *gural* the men agreed to fetch next day. But though we waited till six, only one *tahr* came into sight and he was a long, long way down to the right. A stalk would have taken nearly an hour over that rough and precipitous ground. But, fortunately, through the glasses it could just be seen that he was a young animal with poor horns and the thought of a stalk was at once abandoned. Shortly after six we started to climb back the way we had come and pulled ourselves slowly upwards to the rocks on the crest. As a matter of fact, it was really easier to climb up than to climb down, though more trying to the wind, and, in the cool of the evening, I found myself considerably less tired when I reached the top than I had been at the end of the descent in the heat of the day.

CHAPTER XII.

THE RAMZAN 'ID—THE MOON NOT SEEN—KASHMIRI SUPERSTITION.

THE next day, it was thought, should have been the Ramzan 'Id, the feast which at the end of the Mussulman month of fasting inaugurates the new lunar month. All the members of my following were Mussulmans. It is true they had taken full advantage of the dispensation which exempts travellers from the rigours of the fast, but they were none the less anxiously expectant of the festival. I had sent down to the village for a sheep for their food and had supplied them with sugar for their cooking, and the day was to be spent in rest and in rejoicing. I thought of Hafiz and the first line of one of his more mordant odes, "the fast has gone, the feast has come, and dance we must." But, alas, the next day was after all to bring no rejoicing, let alone dancing—a word of horror to the pious. For the Mussulman calendar is regulated by the moon, and, before a new month can be recognized to have begun, the new moon must have shown herself to the faithful. In more populous regions, the word of a single *mullah* or presbyter is accepted and the telegraph conveys the news of the moon's rising from Bombay in a few minutes to every town and village in the Presidency. But here, alone on a mountain-top, with no communications, we had to rely on our own observation; and not the faintest of silvery gleams could be discerned by the keenest eye among the watchers on the rocks. With sadness they had at last to confess that the crescent was not yet visible—that the feast must be put off for another day.

And truly this 'Id or Feast or Festival, at the end of the bitter fasting of a month, is no mean Holy Day. For, compared to the Fast of Ramzan, Lent is a dim and feeble shadow, a plaything of children in the way of carnal macerations. During Ramzan, for a full four weeks, from dawn to sunset must there be no eating and no drop of water may pass the parched lips nor smoke of tobacco bring respite to the troubled nerves. Dispensation there is only for the sick and for such as are enfeebled by eld and for those that voyage by sea or by land. At night, it is true, they may eat, as they hearken to the homilies of the learned or listen to the word of the Book or the sacred commentaries upon Scripture. Yet even at night, do the pious and sanctified hold that converse between husband and wife in this month of affliction shall be unlawful. In winter, the prescriptions of the Feast are not, perhaps, so terrible: but the lunar months slip quickly round the progression of the sun, and Ramzan must as often fall in the fullness of an Indian summer. And in India, in the hot weather, with the sun ablaze from five in the morning through the weary long hours of the day till he sets in the summer haze at eight, fifteen mortal hours of insufferable flame and a bursting agony of heat, not to sustain the body with any nourishment, not even to slake the intolerable thirst with a drop of water, that is in very deed a torment and anguish of the damned or (much the same after all) of suffering saints. For I at least have never been able to conceive that the damned can undergo more suffering in some contingent hell than the pious and sanctified most really do impose on themselves in this very world of our own. At all events it requires no little fixity of belief and no small strength of will, as of body, to enter on such a deprivation and such lengthy miseries ; and with hunger and thirst to labour and earn bread in the sweat of the brow, as many have to do, even the whole long day, is a task and test that must strain endurance. It is small wonder, therefore, that the 'Id which opens a new month of easy and happy life should be the gayest of all days in the Muslim year, with laughter and bright clean raiment, and eating of pilaus and drinking of sherbets and kisses and hearts' rejoicing. Nor is it to be wondered that there are thousands, aye, hundreds of thousands who sit eagerly watching in the twilight and strain their eyes for the first sight of the new moon.

The Mussalmans of Kashmir are, with a few exceptions, wholly illiterate and, in consequence, are still grossly and absurdly superstitious. They will not eat, for instance, in company with any that be not of the faith nor even partake of food cooked for such a one, though the meat be from an animal slaughtered by a Mussalman butcher after due pronouncement of the ritual formula " In the name of God, the Compassionate, the Merciful." Nay more, I found that, hot and thirsty on a long day's shoot in these exhausting mountains, they would rather do without water than drink it from a bag which had been used by my Indian servant, a Mussalman himself. For they accounted him to be a heretic and a backslider, inasmuch as he ate of what came from his master's table. I argued with them of their folly and showed them that with 'people of the Book'—Christians or Jews who hold to the Scriptures—it was free and lawful to eat and drink, if the meat and drink be not itself unlawful. And I told them that every educated Mussalman in the world and even the ignorant in the more advanced countries of Islam did so eat freely. My *shikari* agreed with me in part and conceded at least that this was, as he understood it, the ordinance of the law. But custom and the fears of superstition are above all reason; and they asserted that the Moulvis of Kashmir, those that are learned in the sacred law, the Pharisees, had denounced such contact and prohibited such common eating. Whether this be an aspersion and a libel on the Moulvis of the land I do not know nor can I discover. I certainly should not, on any grounds of *a priori*, put such anti-heretical pronouncements past them. In all creeds and countries it is obvious that a priesthood must always, as long as it still seems safe, enforce the seclusion of their chosen people. Their authority and the scale of religious values on whose fanciful basis it rests, while they can still persuade people to regard them as valuable realities, can be maintained and confirmed only by the exclusion of that freeër intelligence and that critical comparison which become active on contact with the Gentiles. Hence it is their interest to secure an intellectual *pardah.* As diligent shepherds it is theirs to look to it that the chosen sheep are folded apart from the frisky goats. For truly their horn shall be uplifted, if the people are worshipful and singleminded in their following.

That " new Presbyter is but old Priest writ large " is as true of Islam now as it was in England after the Reformation. The Prophet, indeed, after study of Christianity and of the Rabbis of the Israelites, had, with ample foreknowledge of human events, cried out " In Islam shall be neither priest nor monk." But the pillar of his " No " has been defaced by his descendants and the sacred prohibition is obliterated by the weeds of many centuries. *Darvish* and *Kalandar* and *Faqir* are little better now than the veriest monk, and *Mullah* and *Mujtahid* are of the same breed as any minister or pastor. Moreover, like the tribe of Levi, they have even had the pretension to set up a hereditary caste, and, in the face of the teachings of the Prophet, they have forbidden marriages of their blood with the houses of the people and they mark their peculiar sanctity by distinctions of dress and habit.

For all this, however, I put down the Kashmiri observances in regard to food and drink not directly at least to any priestly admonitions but ultimately to this fact only that the Mussalmans of the valley are all, to a man, descended from Hindu converts to the Faith. What has happened is simply that,as is so often seen in India, the converts when they changed their *credo* still preserved the separatist customs of their Hindu caste. The change has so far at least made for liberality that the Mussulmans of the place mingle and eat bread with each other, though they are sprung originally of different castes. But, as against the world without, they maintain the rigid exclusion of the Hindu system and avoid, as polluting, the touch of the stranger. I have myself eaten with Moors in Algiers from the same dish, and in Bombay of course every Mussalman of the better class will eat with the Christian without thought or hesitation. But where the Mussalman comes of a family converted from the Hindu system and remains uneducated, he is, to this day, strangely reluctant to escape from a rule of conduct shaped, after all, not by his faith, however he may strain its interpretation, but by the influence of his Hindu neighbours and an immemorial tradition from the past. Sometime, perhaps, an enlightened Mussalman of India will with scholarship and impartiality record that fascinating chapter in the development of religions which has to relate the moulding of Islam in India by Hindu pressure, the resulting confusion in the law of succession, the tragic breaches wrought in the admirable marriage-law of the Prophet, the segregation of different communities by trade or descent, and the interpolation of Hindu festivals by different names within the Mussalman calendar.

CHAPTER XIII.

LOOKING FOR TAHR—BUFFALOES IN THE MOUNTAINS—MORE RAIN—MOVING CAMP—AN IMPRESSION OF THE MOUNTAINS.

THE morning of the 21st was again very misty. Though my *shikari* went out, he was unable to see anything at all through the grey clouds and returned early after a fruitless walk. I went for a short stroll on the hill-side with my dog after breakfast and then settled down to write letters, as far as the bees, which all but swarmed in my tent, would give me peace.

By luncheon time the mists had drifted. So, after that meal, I went out with my *shikari* along the ridge to the next mountain-peak and half-way up it to look for *tahr*. Here we could follow a track the whole way, a welcome change from the fatigues of previous days. It was quite a broad track indeed; for the Gujjars drive their cattle this way to the richer grazing found on the farther shoulder of the mountain or down the hill-side, to a ring of trees, half-way down, known as Peri-bagh, the Fairy Garden. When we reached the place most suited for our purpose, I sat down in the shade near the track, while my *shikari* and a coolie clambered down the crags beside me to scout for possible *tahr*

As I sat, I found amusement in watching half-a-dozen bullocks and three buffaloes being driven down the track by two men and a dog. The bullocks managed pretty well, and after all one is used to seeing cows and steers grazing in the uplands of the Swiss Alps also. But one would expect a buffalo on a mountain as little as a fly in amber. Poor brutes, they had a wretched time on the move and it was as pathetic as it was laughable to see them stumbling over stones and their heavy bodies awkwardly contorted at the abrupt angles of the descent. To me it is a never-ending surprise to see these beasts of the plain and the morass uplifted to an altitude of 10,000 foot on some high mountain meadow. Yet I have seen them cross the Rajdiangan pass in snow and ice at 12,000 foot and they seemed not too unhappy. There is, however, an incongruity in their presence among pine-trees and Alpine flowers, which hits one almost like an impropriety. They should be wallowing, after all, in some muddy puddle on a sun-baked plain, their noses just above the water, with a slow tail brushing away the drowzy flies. The buffalo, however, curious though it seems, flourishes thoroughly in his new surroundings. In Kishtwar buffaloes were introduced, I am told, a hundred years ago when the Gujjars first came to the province in the train of its Dogra conquerors. In Kashmir, fifteen years ago, when I first saw the country, they were still unknown. But the Gujjars of the Punjab now bring them every year in thousands into Kashmir and far up the Gilgit Road. For the buffaloes belong to the Gujjars and the Gujjars to their buffaloes. They are bred and kept by no other race in these mountains ; and even in Kishtwar, after a hundred years, they are not to be seen in any Rajput house or with any one except the descendants of their first owners. At any rate, in spite of mountain altitudes, they thrive exceedingly and are fat and strong and lusty ; they give a rich yield of milk; and their calves are sturdy and upstanding. What I like about them, as I meet them often on the hill-side, is that they are friendly, kindly, unsuspicious brutes, very different from the half-wild, wholly-savage beast that meets one too often in the Bombay Deccan. But the Gujjar knows how to treat animals ; he and his woman-folk and his children live and sleep among the cattle, and make pets of each one of them ; and even the stupid buffalo responds to their kindness and looks upon all men as his natural friends. At all events the buffalo has now become a native, if only by naturalization, of these mountains. And some time, perhaps, in the dim future, when civilizations have gone to rest and have again uprisen, a famous osteologist of some now unknown University will, from the evidence of fossil excavations, reconstruct the extinct race of Himalayan wild buffaloes ; and, all unknowing, will owe his reputation for research to the poor ignorant Gujjar of to-day, idly grazing his cattle on the hill-side. Except for the passing of the cattle, I had nothing to do while I waited and it was quite a pleasant excitement to see a small snake creep from beside my foot. I killed it at once with my stick and, from the shape of its head, took it to be some kind of viper. But of *tahr* there was no news. Three females alone could be sighted and we had to return home with nothing to our credit. The evening was beautiful; the mountains opposite more clear and seeming nearer than ever; and the sickle of the new moon just palely visible about a foot above the western mountains.

But the fine evening forecast a wretched sequence. It poured in the night, and the morning was raw and misty. During most of the day we were in the midst of thick cloud and we could hardly see a dozen yards in front of us. When, for a few minutes at a time, a wisp of cloud blew away, we had the sorry consolation of seeing it rain across the valley; but very soon the brief glimpse would again be veiled by a fresh mist. To go out shooting was of course hopeless, for the eye could certainly not penetrate the fog, to even the nearest possible distance for a shot. I went for a short walk twice and spent the rest of the day in reading. By evening, however, the air became clearer, and at seven I took my rifle and walked to the nearest *gural* ground, only fifteen minutes away, on the off-chance that, by extraordinary luck, I might find a possible shot. But off-chances are the chances that do not come *off*: and the only benefit I got from the walk was a healthy glow and reasonable exercise before dinner.

The next day, the 23rd, we were to move camp halfway down the hill to try there for bear; for my time was drawing to its close and I still wanted to add a bearskin or two to my bag. We left in rain which had begun in the middle of the night and was to last, as it happened, for another day and a half without a break. To move camp is at best a melancholy business, though a small tent and a few carriers do not bring that peculiar feeling of sadness which in India is carried in the night hours by the many carts, and the lowing of cattle, and the deep slow notes of their bells and the view of a dismantled encampment. In Kishtwar my camp was at its barest minimum and could be broken up in an hour with ease. But to move in rain, to stand shivering under the poor shelter of a tree and watch the coolies crouching beside a wretched fire, while the last loads were got ready, was a cheerless business and a reminder of human mutability. And now that my face was set down-hill and towards the homeward march, I knew full well that I was saying my last good-bye to the higher peaks of Kishtwar and the chamois and wild-goats of the Himalayas. The information I had looked for had not come from Pambar and there seemed no sufficient hopes of ibex to justify the long and hurried march. On the other hand, so much of my time had been wasted by the bad weather we had had that it seemed impracticable to try more than to hunt bear on the lower slopes. I felt, therefore, that I was now looking my last from the higher altitudes upon this land of mountains. It was unlikely, as far as I could forecast my life, that I should ever again be able to penetrate this corner of the Himalayas, and I knew that, as the years advanced, it would be impossible again to tempt these crags and stern declivities.

Yet, take it all in all, these mountains do not really take one to their heart. They are too vast, too ubiquitous, too overwhelming. They have in them a certain—what the Latins called—immanity—a brutal massivity, an inhuman Titanism. Their outline, their mass, their morphology, one feels, must have been just so, as they now still stand, unchanged, from the primeval age when the earth first vomited forth the formations of the earlier æons from her chaotic bubbling crust. They are earlier than life and antecedent to the first desires of the just living cysts and cells. They do not draw and allure; they overpower. In their details they are often beautiful, in the most exact sense of the word lovely. The sight of wild-flowers in a coloured legion, the white birches between the pines, the unforgettable scent of deodars drying in the hot sun after a shower, the ferns under a little cataract, the ripple and splash of the lesser rivulets, the cool bracing touch of the air, these are the memories of the great hills that shall always remain, loved and revivifying. The details —yes—but in the mass—they are repressive, a little terrifying, a little tiring.

Perhaps the fact is, that for the full charm of mountain scenery is needed the contrast of smiling valleys and the blue refreshment of placid lakes. It is in this, in the outstretched fertile vale, the slow broad river and the great spreading lake, as well as the contours of its wooded rounded hills and the snowy summits of its more distant mountains, that Kashmir finds with its perpetual variety its enduring fascination. Switzerland, too, has with and among its Alps innumerable broadly-curving valleys and gardens and the habitations of men and deep pasture-lands and the endless charm of its many lakes.

But in Kishtwar there is only one small plateau—that on which the town itself is placed—and there are no valleys. What there are, are mere clefts, deep narrow rocky gorges, between beetling bewildering mountain masses. Often the rocky foundations of the monstrous heights rise sheer and straight from the torrent at the bottom and for hundreds of feet two rival Titans of cliff threaten each other, separated only by the same unchanging and limited space. On the face of the wall of rock a tortuous path, a foot or two wide, just finds itself room to cling. In other places the gorge may so far widen till there be room for a miserable hut or two, backed against the slighter slope, to be reared above a few terraced fields each less than a dozen paces across. But general cultivation has to be scattered further up higher on the hill-side, where, above the first straightness of the ravine, the mountains here and there yield a small patch of land less steep, more compromising. They make only a few thin patches, here and there, these cottages and those maize-fields, one-third of the way up perhaps on the hill, against the monumental vastness of these tremendous upheavals. For man is here reduced to the lowest power against an immoveable monotony of stony nature. In it all is too little of human significance, too great a humiliation. For us at least, in this our generation, the feeling is unfriendly, unsympathetic. The world has had enough, Heaven knows, of man's humiliation and of a cowardly prostration before the uncontrolled forces of nature in the last seventeen centuries, since the spirit of old Greece was routed and the proud '*homo sum*' of Rome was whelmed under unmanly lamentations for our miserable 'mortal flesh.' Once, it is true, for one cheerful wholesome moment, the breath of clean, virile life did fill the lungs of the unshackled Renaissance: but too soon, alas, was it again stifled in the close-shuttered chambers of ignorance and supernatural fears and a base humility. And now we, in our time and age, need light and breadth and a cheerful humanity and the sense of power and a friendly unity with the whole living animal world of which we are only one part, perhaps the most conscious of ourselves and of our powers. We find this sympathy, with the added beauty of wild things, in a hill-country, in Scotland for instance when the slopes are purple under heather and each scurrying cloud gives a modifying shade and seems to alter the very curves and contours of the moorland.

Or in broad plains, stretching unfenced, unhedged before the dreamy eye to be lost in the vague horizon, one is still in sympathy, united, sentient, unoppressed, with the illimitable infinity of the transfluent universe. On such vast plains one knows the temporal impermanence of man and feels perhaps a little lost, a little melancholy; but he who stands and looks into their unbounded span is still one with the procession of the earth, and can aspire further to traverse their infinite extension. He dreams himself into a passionless acquiescence in the unknown flux of which he is one focus, for one moment conscious.

But these grim, stark mountains without room to live or till or reap, without variety, stern and unbending, are to man an antagonism and a material hostility, from which even their hypocritical forests can not quite redeem them.

CHAPTER XIV.

CHANGE OF CLIMATE—A BEAR SEEN—I MOVE CAMP—SPORTING SUPERSTITIONS.

It was in rain that we left our camp and descended from the meadow among the rocks to the deodar forests, and through the forests to the Gujjar huts and from their settlement to a fine grove of pine-trees beside the uppermost limits of cultivation. On the way we passed the clearing where my tents had formerly been pitched and sat there a few minutes resting in the dripping rain. Fortunately among the pine-trees the ground was carpeted with dry pine-needles and had hardly begun to grow wet. The tents could therefore be pitched and occupied in comfort. During the descent, though it was little more than a thousand foot from the summit, the change of climate had been astonishing, as great, say, as from Braemar to the Riviera on a rainy day. In this showery weather, the new warmth was agreeable and I felt more hopeful of fine days in this balmier air.

In spite of fitful rain in the afternoon, I went out to look for a bear—the same animal that had given me the chance which I had failed to take. Beside the pine-grove where I had camped were three or four of those small cultivated terraces which pass for fields in

Kishtwar. Beyond those, there was a thick patch of scrub-jungle, about one mile square, on a slope. I could see that it was thickly overgrown with bushes but it was only as I forced my way through that I felt that most of them were thorny. Among them, however, was also a number of guelder-berry bushes, which were the great attraction to the bear. On the further side of this scrub-jungle was a fairly thick forest of pines with very heavy undergrowth.

In the early afternoon I got word that a man had seen the bear reclining in a more or less open clearing just inside this pine-forest. I went, accordingly, with my *shikari* through the scrub-jungle in that direction, as silently as we could. But in ground so over-grown that one's way has to be forced, step by step, with a struggle through clinging thicket and where, moreover, every few minutes the foot slips into some concealed hole or trips over some disobliging stone, it is impossible to attain any real silence. We, therefore, did not dare to go too close to the place in the pine-forest where the bear was reported to be lying. For, if he were once frightened by a sound, it might be days before he returned again. Thus, though we went as near as we dared in the hope of catching a sight of the bear, we had to leave off, when we could not see him in the border of the forest. We, therefore, went back a little way, as silently as we had come, and sat on a high rock a short distance up the hill, from which we could command as satisfactory a view as the circumstances allowed over the whole piece of scrub-jungle. We sat there a long time without seeing a sign of the bear and in the meantime the rain began to drip and finally to pour. In the downpour I gave it up and returned to my tent wet and cold and bad-tempered.

While I was having dinner, the third panther whose distant acquaintance I had formerly made, came close to us and obliged with a musical treat outside my tent. I tied up my dog hastily and went out to look for my spotted friend. But the night was so dark that it was hopeless to try to see him, and in a few minutes a growl further down the hill convinced me that he had gone to lower levels to hunt for his meal. As a precaution, however, I had a fire lit outside my tent; and I was very glad for my own dog's sake that I had done so when, before falling asleep, I heard from a distance that one shrill immediately-silenced yelp of a dog which always proclaims the sudden snatch and the sudden death. Next morning I was told that the panther had pounced on a shepherd's dog and carried him off to eat.

Though the next day opened with rain, it had cleared up by the afternoon and I tried my luck again with the bear, sitting on the same rock as the previous day. This time I did see the bear. I caught a glimpse of him, that is to say, at about four hundred yards passing from one bush to another. Hoping that he would move upwards in our direction, we waited for ten or fifteen minutes where we were. But no other movement followed and we had to decide to try and track him through the scrub. For the next hour and a half we fought and scratched our way through thorns and bushes and over stones and rocks. We saw plenty of marks and we penetrated two masses of bush which evidently by all the signs were his habitual lairs. But he himself remained invisible. Perhaps he had moved on elsewhere. More probably, I feared, he was still lurking under some bush that we had failed to examine fully and carefully and was laughing at us and our efforts in the broad-mouthed rolling rollicking way that bears have. He had the best of it anyway and had the right to laugh last. When I got home, vexed and tired, I swore in three languages that nothing should again tempt me after this fellow—the phantom bear I would have christened him, had I not seen, yea, and forgone, his all too solid flash.

Wednesday, the 25th of July, was at last a beautiful sunny day. The caretaker of the Ziarat or shrine of Zain-ul-Din lower down the hill to the north-west had let me know the previous evening of a bear that had been eating his apricots. I had, therefore, decided to move in that direction to a camping-ground beyond the shrine, when I should both be near to the apricot-munching animal and also to a nallah where I hoped for a successful beat. But the transport coolies did not turn up till nearly one o'clock, and then only after I had walked down-hill and had a few words with the village headman. We had, therefore, to move in the heat of the day, and the day was very hot. The march was anything but pleasant. But I rested on the way in the apricot-garden of the Ziarat and had a long talk with the caretaker, himself a sprout on the saint's tree. I had given him another silver offering and he was gracious to a degree.

From this holy man I heard more of the sporting superstitions of the country. But to him the lore that he disclosed was made up of credences worthy to be accepted and propositions of a fair induction. I had already known that the Kishtwari, like the Bhil of the Satpuras and Central India, believes that if the tongue of a slain animal hang out between the teeth to one side of the mouth, it is a good augury for the success of the next shoot. The last panther I had shot had its tongue hanging in this position, and upon the sign, every one had promised me infallible luck on the next occasion.

Why this opinion should be held both by the Bhil and the Kishtwari, I do not know, unless it throws back to some long-forgotten common Dravidian origin of belief, if not of race. At any rate both peoples are at one in crediting the unfortunate dying animal with some sort of dumb, miraculous swan-song of prophecy; though why the poor brute should be compelled to gratify its own murderer by a favourable omen at that last painful moment, they do not attempt to conjecture. Another equally well-grounded belief is that some panthers have a claw at the end of their tail, in order apparently that they should have a longer reach in attack. But as far as I could make out, these ungula-caudiferous leopards, like old soldiers, never die but simply fade away. At least, with all my enquiries, I could never hear of anyone who had ever met any one who had ever heard of anyone else who had seen such an animal shot or dead.

The old gentleman of the Ziarat however, reached even rarer heights. For, in the presence of his acquiescent and applauding followers, he assured me that he himself, *ipse ipsissimus*, had with these very eyes,—how could they be mistaken ?—seen the leopard only two nights ago, ere ever he made off with the dog, go circling three times round his saintship's garden and watched him prostrate himself there several times, forehead in dust, before the latch and lintel of the sainted shrine. His obeisance fulfilled and accomplished, the adoring leopard had in all reverence departed—and killed a dog. With an eye on the admiring countenances of his disciples, I made an effort to compress my larynx and without the least vestige of a gurgle, murmured the polite offering of an awestruck "wāh! wāh!"—"wonderful, wonderful." Thus encouraged, the pious sacristan went on to tell how his respected ancestor, in whatever resurrected form he has chosen to make his home in these desolate hills, is master of all the beasts of the forest. All of them show him respect and open veneration. In particular to his own certain knowledge and constant observation, *Kasm-i-Khuda*,—by God I swear it—every Thursday night and every Friday evening, before the Sabbath prayers and after their completion, the leopard comes in worshipful silence to the shrine and in his dumb bestial way performs his prayers by prostration. Thereafter he can roam, with the saint's blessing on his head, through the village outskirts and carry off the fat sheep or straying bullock of a neighbour. To my infidel mind, I must confess; the saint's blessing seemed a trifle misplaced and his favour to the leopard a little hard on the owner of sheep or steer, and even harder perhaps on the wretched victim of his unkind kindness. But then, I suppose, all benevolences and indulgences and the like from saints and similar nuisances who interfere by way of providential interposition with the infinite chain of cause and effect must, like other hard cases, go to make bad law and impair the reasoned foundations of eternal justice.

My Indian servant, I was glad to notice, had enough of a sceptical turn at once to seize the same argument about sheep and owner. But it was met, in quite modern theo-philosophical style, by a Gujjar of the place whose name, if it was not Eucken, deserved to be and who in any case would have been at home in an up-to-date, advanced Protestant pulpit. This Gujjar had no hesitation in constructing a rationalistic basis for faith, quite as good as any other, in the current manner. For, he explained, in every case the kid, sheep, or steer of course belonged to a sinful man who had failed to make a due offering at the shrine. In this way, it would be seen, the saint combined a true paedagogic care for good morals, in other words, the interests of his descendants at the shrine, with a merely reasonable favour to the devout leopard. Of course this pious reasoning still left out of account the feelings of the sheep and its family. But then, I suppose, one cannot expect everything from such arguments. They must be difficult enough, God knows, to bring as far as they are brought, and a little lameness is easily overlooked by a willing congregation.

At the first sight I had been disappointed at coming so close to the shrine; for, seen so near, the building itself was after all tawdry and poor. The romantic grace which had impressed me at a distance, far down the hill-side, was lost in the detailed view. But now I felt that the disappointment was amply paid for by these new lights on Kishtwari thought. After all, when even in modern France fashionable persons and the would-be fashionable have their hounds blessed and perform the ritual of St. Hubert for the chase, the credulities of Kishtwar are as entitled to stir kinship as mere ridicule.

CHAPTER XV.

SITTING UP FOR BEAR—THREE FRUITLESS BEATS—A BAD CLIMB—FATIGUE—A KISHTWARI GLOSSARY.

I WENT on after my talk at the Ziarat and found my camp. It was getting late by this time and, as soon as I had had tea, I returned with my rifle to the garden beside the shrine. Here, by the light of the new moon, I sat up long after sunset waiting for the bear to come back for another feast on the apricots. But this was evidently not his night and at last, when the moon was sinking behind the mountains, I had to return disappointed to my belated dinner. It was more than annoying to hear next morning that this very bear had in broad daylight, before ever the sun had set, gone to some other apricot trees only half-a-mile away and had there gorged himself with the fruit in full sight of several men, none of whom had had enough intelligence to run over and inform me at the time.

The next day, the 26th, was again sunny and hot. As the sun neared its meridian, I set out to climb a steep Kishtwari hill, and to perspire profusely, on my way to a beat which I had been promised would prove a certain find. The beaters, I was assured by the sportsman of the place, Laldin, were good men who would never let a bear slip away, and a bear there would assuredly be in this wood above the maize-fields. The last words I uttered as I parted from the beaters were, "Now, Laldin, remember that the beat must on no account start till I got to my place and whistle." And he had replied with a willing and acquiescent, "Ha, Jinab "—"Assuredly, Oh! Threshold "—the polite equivalent in Hindustani of the German 'Serenity', I suppose. But I was still climbing through the forest, nearly a quarter of a mile from my place, when I suddenly heard a frenzied yell of "Here's the bear", followed by a hurricane of calls from the beaters, scattered in a disorderly rabble through the lower fringes of the jungle. It was only too clear that, in their excitement, they had broken into a sort of go-as-you-please beat at the first silly shriek of the man who had seen the bear and lost his own head. In the place where I happened to be at that moment, I could barely see ten yards on either side and I fancied there was in any case little prospect of the bear coming up in that line. On the other hand it seemed hopeless to make for my own point now in the hurry. But where else was I to go? I climbed at last to a little eminence which gave me a slightly better line of vision, though even here I had little hope of the bear's coming. For sometime I could hear the beaters going on making an absurd uproar in a disorderly and broken line. They seemed to be coming a little nearer me when the shouting stopped as suddenly as it had begun. It seemed to me, when they stopped, that I might perhaps run across to my real place, before they began beating again. But as I reached the first corner on the road, what was my disgust to find that some of the stops or beaters—heaven alone knows which—had actually come up and occupied the very place where I was to have sat and to which the beat was to be directed. To go there now was, therefore, out of the question and the only thing I could do (and that little better than useless) was to go back again to the hillock to which I had rushed at the beginning. I got back; shouts began again; and slowly the beaters worked their way up, in nothing like a line, some in front, others a long way behind, most of them anywhere but where they should have been. Without exception it was the very worst beat I had ever seen. The bear had of course not come up and, after wearying cross-examination by my *shikari*, it was found that, on being first disturbed, he had quietly walked out to the right hand of the beat between two stops who had not stopped him. I also discovered that these famous beaters, whom Laldin had so highly extolled, had never been in a beat before and that Laldin himself was in the same blissful state of ignorance.

That I was furious at all this muddle, needs no saying; and I wanted to go home at once—if I may call my little tent home. However, the men entreated and protested and my *shikari* spoke soothing words; and I was at last, most foolishly, persuaded to try two more beats to the right of where we had been. All the men assured me with one voice that these patches of jungle were small and that the bear could have gone only to them and that in one of the two beats he must certainly be come at. I yielded and agreed to try. It was hot enough already, one of those typical still Kishtwari days, when it is oppressive on the lower slopes of the mountains and no breeze blows to give an instant's relief from the intense heat. The next beat was far too close to the last and was in my opinion hopeless from the start. When it was over, I had something to eat and felt better in spite of the trying temperature.

I was now at the nearer side of the patch of jungle destined for the next beat—a square piece about a mile across, directly above the *ziarat*. There were no real trees in it but it was thickly overgrown with bush. The point where I was to sit was on the other side about a mile away and I started to walk towards it through the scrub. But Laldin at once called to me and said that the bushes would make the direct line very troublesome. He advised me to take a track that went up the hill, which, he said, would bring me down easily on the other side to my place. This should, I think, have aroused my suspicions but, as I had little hopes of the beats, I was by now indifferent and did not pay much attention to the circumstances. On the track which I now followed, the climb up was a little trying, not on account of any particular steepness but because of the great heat. But from the top along the ridge and then down to my point the walking was at this stage of the day really terrible. I found myself obliged to clamber down rocks and force my way through thorns, to watch every step, to jump and, at places, even to crawl. Long before I reached my point, there was not a dry stitch on my body, and I felt almost ill from the incessant perspiration. I could not even turn back, for to do so meant facing the same difficulties again with a steep ascent into the bargain. When I at last reached the crag where I was to sit, I was worn-out, tired, and bored with the whole business. The beat began ; but it needed only a minute or two to see that it was bound to be useless. The beaters were only twenty-five in all ; and they were supposed to work through a square mile of thorn and thicket, though many parts of which a man could hardly force his way and many places in which were impenetrable to the eye. The bear, I now found, could lie anywhere in this jungle and be passed unseen and unnoticed. And this was of course exactly what happened. That the bear was there, I am ready to believe, and, from all the circumstances, think extremely probable. But either he did not move or, if he did, he moved quietly and unperceived under thick bushes. By no possibility could he be seen either by me or by the beaters. The beat drew to a straggling end without sight of any animal.

The sorry business at last over, I had still to climb down and the only possible way, a very bad one, led me further and further from my encampment. We had to get down and strike the road from the main village to the *ziarat*, before we could turn to the right on the homeward route. I got back after six, absolutely tired out, chiefly on account of the terrific heat which had been almost as hot as an Indian summer and at least as still. I could only fling myself on my bed like a log and lie still, till I revived myself with several cups of tea. Then I gave orders for an early start next morning on the return march to Kashmir. I had to be back at

Islamabad on the 5th of August and I had had no fur ther news from Pambar. The idea of trying for ibex had therefore to be given up, much as I regretted the conclusion. The only course that seemed to be still open was to start at once and thereby leave myself three days to try for bear in the upper valleys of Kashmir on the other side of the pass from Kishtwar.

By the way some one should really write a glossary of the meanings of Hindustani words as used in Kishtwar by the inhabitants. It would, I feel sure, be a help and a solace to many and it could hardly fail to be amusing, whenever the reader was not too tired to enjoy the point. Thus '*sadak,*' for instance, in Hindustani a 'high road,' means in Kishtwari usage a footpath between six inches and a foot wide, in which there are not more than two really dangerous places per mile. But it is of course always *high,* though not a *road.* *Maidan,* in Hindustani an open level space or meadow, is used here for an acclivity at an angle of about 80 degrees, without large trees, but thickly covered with small rocks and impenetrable scrub. *Asaniki jaga,* which in Hindustani would be ground to be covered with ease and facility, here conveys the description of a situation in which with ordinary luck you are unlikely to break your neck and should get off readily with a broken leg or dislocated thigh. The sporting scholar, I am sure, could collect many hundreds of instances of such peculiar dialectic usage. To these hardy hill-men of course the connotation they attach to the phrases is quite natural. For they have never had a level foot of earth to walk on. From their first crawl in infancy every step they take is either up or down a slope sufficiently steep to be inconvenient or even perilous to the unaccustomed stranger. This constant exertion may perhaps account for the prematurely aged look of everyone in the province. One does not see a single person who looks as if he could be anything between sixteen and forty. For as soon as they have ceased to be mere boys, the people seem to develop by one stride into wrinkled, middle-aged, tired men. It is true, of course, everywhere that country-folk age with terrible rapidity. Dirt and insanitary conditions, mental vacuity and stagnation are enough to account for this in an ordinary way. It is only in the large towns, with their careful cleanliness, their variety, their amusements and manifold interests, in a London, a Paris, or a Vienna, that human beings can hope to remain younger than their years and trust that their days will be long, not merely in number but also by the well-filled account of their activities. It is also true that in all countries the lower classes age more quickly and definitely than the upper. It is sometimes alleged that this is due to their harder labour, but without truth or reason. The farm labourer in the year works much less hard than the skilled artisan and wastes much more time in vacuous idleness. The work of neither can be compared for a moment to the con stant toil of the educated professional man. Even a civil servant works harder than the so-called working-man. But they have less real ease and a lower standard of comfort ; in particular they are less attentive to that greatest of all aids to youth, a scrupulous cleanliness. And the unchanging fixity of the face in an uneducated person, who thinks little and feels very few emotions, undoubtedly creates those early and deep wrinkles, which are so often the mark and feature of the common man. The face of the educated man, on the other hand, is always mobile. The lines alter from moment to moment with the quick-changing thought and the rapid emotions which pursue each other across his words ; and this constant play of facial muscle tends to erase or at any rate to lighten the lines which would otherwise be graven on his skin by the accumulating years. But in Kishtwar the marks of age are earlier and deeper than among the peasantry of another country. Mere dirt, mere ignorance, mere stagnation are not enough to account for such premature deterioration. The lines are like those which the instantaneous camera reveals on the face of the runner who has won a distance-race. I think, therefore, that their special explanation lies in the incessant effort of mountain-climbing and the bitter labour of inhalation on those heights. That the Kishtwaris who attain to mature age do so only by the survival of the fittest, seems to be certain. They themselves admit, though they do so reluctantly as if they were putting a slight on their motherland, that a certain number among them find a sudden end by a slip of the foot on some treacherous cliff. It is a real dispensation that the use of liquor is unknown in Kishtwar, where even in their religious ceremonial the Rajputs use no libations to the *soma*-drinking Indra. One St. Andrew's Night dinner in Kishtwar would more than decimate the male population ; and a course of free-masonry, should lodges ever be founded ***in hac petra***, would mean the literal dilapidation of the province.

CHAPTER XVI.

SHOOTING IN KISHTWAR—THE BEST SEASON—THE RETURN MARCH—THE EVIL EYE—A HOT MARCH—TUGUD.

NEXT morning I set my face, I cannot say towards home (for the road led for miles in the directly opposite direction), but at least on the homeward way. I had said my last good-bye, no doubt for life, to shooting in Kishtwar. For it was in every way unlikely that fate should again have in store for me an opportunity of visiting at least the remoter and less accessible portions of the Himalayas.

I had had an experience which I should be sorry to have missed; had secured specimens of animals difficult to obtain, of which the numbers living are not large and their homes remote and circumscribed; and had stayed in the middle of scenery much of which was very beautiful and all unusual, unexpected, perhaps unique. My total bag was of course small. In three weeks I had secured one *tahr*, three *gural* or chamois, and two panthers. To this I could have added a bear and should have added another *gural*, had everything been for the best. This can hardly be called successful shooting, though I have known more time spent in Kashmir on getting a poorer bag. But I had come to

Kishtwar deliberately, with full knowledge of the fact, at the worst shooting season.

For the sportsman as such the best season is from the middle of April to the end of May; the second best is September. During the former period snow and cold weather drive the wild-goats and chamois to the lower slopes of these savage mountains; they group more together; grass is scanty and the animals are easily seen; every condition combines to make successful shooting as easy as it can ever be at animals who live in the wildest of rocky places. The *tahr* is the most difficult to come near of any Himalayan animal except the *markhor*, but in April and May a good climber in his youth should probably be able to count on bagging the four heads which he is allowed by the terms of his license.

Gural, though they live in the same ground as *tahr*, live also on the easier fringes of the precipices and can therefore be more readily got at. In their case the main difficulty is to see them, as owing to their small size they are often completely hidden by the high grass of the summer. In spring they would appear clearly against the small young grass. In September on the other hand the rutting season begins and the *tahr* come out more openly on the lower slopes in pursuit of their caprine loves; and can even be called — an unsporting dodge, I think—by dropping a stone down a rock surface, as if another of their kind were passing there. In September, therefore, the sportsman should easily make a good bag of *tahr*, though the high grass will still interfere with his shooting *gural*. And both in spring and autumn bear are more easily located, than in the height of summer when their movements vary from day to day, almost from hour to hour. These were facts of which I was not wholly ignorant. In a broad sense I knew that in deciding to spend July in Kishtwar, I was certainly sacrificing no small amount of sporting chances. But there were other considerations which decided and had to decide me. Some of those were not personal to myself. Among purely personal considerations, the most important was that the state of my health when I came to Kashmir on leave at the beginning of May put it quite out of the question for me to attempt so trying a journey at so cold a season and in fact to go anywhere any distance beyond a doctor's reach. And in September (supposing I were not recalled from leave of which I did not feel any too certain), I hoped in company with my wife to camp in some near valley in Kashmir for the far easier, but on the whole more enjoyable, pursuit of the stag and the brown bear. Other considerations which, I think, should also obtain due weight from anyone are, first, that the country is of course infinitely more beautiful in the height of summer than it is in spring and perhaps more than it would be in autumn: and second, that July is the month in which the happy valley of Kashmir is at its worst and hottest and in which most visitors want to go away somewhere. Now Kishtwar is of course not cool; its gorges are in fact far hotter than anything in Kashmir. But once arrived on the shooting grounds, the air is quite as cold as one could wish. It is only a matter after all of facing three or four bad days each way on the journeys. And where is the sportsman to go in Kashmir at that season? at least with any hope of obtaining any of the rarer trophies? The best he could do in Kashmir itself would be to look for *serow*, but of those rare animals only one head may be shot. It is all very well for those who can face the extreme climate of Ladakh and spare time for the long journey. But to others it may happen, as it did to me, that the doctor absolutely forbids Ladakh, even though the shooting there presents few of the difficulties which have to be met in Kishtwar. To be reduced to playing golf at Gulmarg or something of the sort would surely be an unfortunate way of wasting a holiday in Kashmir. So to me at any rate a trip to Kishtwar, even with the smaller chance of a good bag, seemed the happiest solution. And I have had no reason to regret the decision. I met perhaps rather an undue amount of rain. But, this being excepted, I saw most beautiful country at its very best and enjoyed flowers and fruit at their most flourishing season.

The one real offset was undoubtedly the heat of the marches. On the way in from Kashmir I had been lucky and it was only one day and a half which could seriously be called trying. I was now to experience what the heat of Kishtwar can really mean to travellers on the march.

We left on the 27th of July at a very early hour. I was called before dawn and dressed and ate my first breakfast by the light of a candle—a horrid proceeding which all my life I have regarded with utter detestation. I have indeed always been a faithful believer in the good old adage,

'Early to rise and early to bed
Makes a man priggish and gives him swell'd head.'

But here, day after day till we had crossed well into Kashmir, the height of the thermometer imposed this early stand to arms, not only, indeed not mainly, for my own sake but above all for the sake of the coolies who had my kit to carry.

By about six-thirty we were on the road, going downhill on a rough track, through lush grass, heavy with dew, and through wet clinging crops of maize. A new bridge, we were told, had been built over the Wardwan river just under our last camp, and we had only to cross that bridge and ascend a little to the south to reach the village opposite, hardly, it seemed, more than a long stone's throw away, where we should spend the night. It was an easy march, it seemed, hardly enough for the day's work, one should think. So we went down and down, a good many hundred foot, in a direct line till we found ourselves turning to go down further to the north-west. Still we went down, and at last we met the considerable track that joins the main Chenab valley with Dachin in the Wardwan Nallah. Here some villagers, who had accompanied us so far, took their leave with polite wishes. It was only later that it struck me that they had perhaps left us here, those villagers who had assured us of the nearness of the bridge, because they found me growing worried at not seeing it appear. But they again assured me that we had only to walk further along the Dachin road—of course in the direction opposite to our ultimate destination—to see it straight below and go down the hill to the crossing. Off we started accordingly on the Dachin road, my *shikari*, my Indian servant, the tiffin-coolie from whom I never let myself be parted and my dog who will never part from me. As there was just a possibility of *gural* being sighted on some rocks about half-a-mile ahead, the *shikari* took my rifle from its case and carried it on his shoulder.

Here by the way I learnt of still another superstition, by asking why the rifle had been packed in its case that morning. The Kishtwar women, it appeared, are credited with the taint of witchcraft. That the women of Tibet are all kent witches, I knew of course before, for their evil name is spread throughout Central Asia and finds place in the poetry of Persia. But I had not yet heard this of the Kishtwar women nor could I from their appearance have guessed their pact with the Evil One. For they are marked neither by inexorable ugliness nor by that exquisite loveliness which in the ages of real religious faith appear to have been the decisive tests of demonic possession, when the ministers of a persecuted Kirk kept the fires flaming and were free to cast such miserable brands to the burning. Nevertheless, my companions assured me, the Kishtwari women are in very truth just such besom-riding, sabbath-breaking succubi of Satan. Among their other powers they have the evil eye. So if such a one should but so much as see my rifle, she would infallibly overlook it, so that every shot should be deflected and my straightest aim end in a miss. Better overlook than overlay, I thought to myself, with some remembrance of our own East Ends and before my eyes the healthy children of these satanical women of Kishtwar. *Non angli sed diaboli pulcri*, I had almost murmured, a second Gregory.

So the rifle came out of its case now and we marched on along the Dachin road. We saw no *gural* of course. But what was worse was that we saw no bridge, even after walking a couple of miles further to the North. What we then met was a mighty cliff, some hundreds of foot high, up which the track, and we with it, had to climb at an angle more steep than agreeable. The heat made itself felt acutely, for no breeze entered the gorge and the sun blazed down on the bare rocks. The climb up the cliff was not one to be readily forgotten. And even from the top we could make out no sign of bridge or crossing. But, after another mile or so, we at last saw a village at a bend in the stream and guessed that the bridge might be beside it round the corner. Even now it was not clear how we were to reach the village. At last we fell in with a traveller, some way on, and he pointed to a wilderness of bush in front and told us we should find a footpath through the bushes. It was a steep and slippery path, when we found it, which zig-zagged all the way down over loose shale, with the sun hotter than ever and still no breath of wind. But we did reach the village at last and a kind old gentleman and his son conducted us over some rocks which were his lawn and over the roofs of two houses to another footpath that led to the long-sought bridge.

By this time we were all done up, not so much by sheer fatigue as by the intense heat. My dog and I were perhaps the most tired, as we were the most susceptible to the sun. There were now five miles left of upward climb in the opposite direction on the other side, before we should reach Tugud, where we were to camp. That side of the gorge had been exposed to the sun without an atom of shade since the first break of dawn, while a glance at the sun's position showed that it would be in shadow by about five-thirty or six in the evening. I, therefore, firmly declined to move another step till that hour and proposed to spend the day at the river's edge dodging after shade from one bush to another.

Here, however, I found real treasure trove. For opposite, on the other bank, some forest contractor had built a shed or store-house for his wood and kindly left it unlocked for the benefit of the weary traveller. There was even a little annexe, a tiny, rather dirty room, which boasted a table and the greater part of a chair. Here I at once installed myself. My *shikari* said, after some hesitation and in the face of my protests, that he would go on with the coolies and my kit when they arrived. I told him, therefore, that I should keep my servant, the tiffin-coolie and my dog with me, and that my bedding was to be laid out on the floor of the shed and the man who carried it detained beside us, when the transport had arrived. I ate my meagre luncheon and by the time I had finished, the coolies came and my bedding was laid out. I lay down and read a few lines but the book dropped out of my hands at once and I found myself falling asleep, a testimony to the fatigue induced by the overpowering heat. My servant and the coolies did the same, but then they are accustomed to easy sleep in the middle of the day. About five I awoke and had tea, and as soon as my followers had had theirs, we set off on the upward path. It was still hot, but by no means unbearable, and we reached our destination in fairly good style, though still a little tired. But the unfortunate *shikari* and the coolies who had gone ahead had had a terrible time and looked, all of them, thoroughly exhausted.

CHAPTER XVII.

A VISHNU TEMPLE—ANTIQUE WELLS—KISHTWARI HEAD-GEAR—A HOT NIGHT—A TIRING MARCH—SINGPUR—CAMP ON THE PASS.

THE village of Tugud is prettily situated and it is pleasant to see many rills of water trickling through the fields and down the hill-side. My tent had been pitched just beside a little wooden temple, dedicated, as they seldom are, to Vishnu. The friendly *chokidar* or village policeman at once unlocked the door, when he saw me strolling round it, and invited me to look in. There was no idol in the temple, but, in place of it, a small stone slab with a much defaced alto-relief of the deity, probably, I imagine, an antique carving from some former, now ruined, edifice. On the floor of the temple were innumerable iron tridents in miniature, the votive offerings of the people. The roof was surmounted by a leopard, carved with much force and grotesque vigour, which, I was told, had been made a few years ago by a travelling artisan from the Punjab. Whoever he was, he had evidently taken delight in his work, may his shadow never grow less, and had the makings of a real artist.

At Tugud there were, what I had previously found in Katan, two or three ancient wells or springs which showed undoubted traces of Greek feeling. They were really buildings, consisting of a wall at the back, with a roof, and pillars to support it at the side and front. The water ran from a spout coming from a sort of stone rosette in the centre of the back wall. The rosette itself was of a conventional Indian pattern. But the architecture of the flat roof and the pillars were of a form that was purely Grecian. These stone-built wells were of considerable size and must have been costly to erect. Any work of the kind would be, all other considerations disregarded, quite beyond the means of any population now existing, or that can conceivably for many centuries past have existed in the province as we know it. They can have been raised by no population of scattered peasants, finding a precarious livelihood in the forests and on the stony mountains. When they were erected, it is obvious that there must have been some other, far superior civilization which had at least its outposts in this mountainous region and which was permeated by Grecian influences. We know enough of the Sáka monarchies of Northern India, to recognize this friendly intercourse with the Ionian Greeks, the Yávans as they were called in the ancient language, and that their power at one time reached through the Himalayan ranges as far as the Lob-Nor desert on the Chinese frontier. The valley of the Chenab and the Kishtwar province is on the direct route from the Panjáb to Ladákh and Turkestan. It is, therefore, a feasible conjecture that in the Sáka era in Kishtwar as in Chamba there may have been Government establishments and garrisons, perhaps even mercantile emporia, of sufficient importance to deserve the expenditure of public money on their commodity and embellishment. It is at least pleasing to conjecture that in those fine erections, extant in the humble villages of poor hill peasants, the eye looks upon the relics of the vanished empire of the Sáka rulers of the sixth century in India and the Trans-Himalaya.

It was happily appropriate that the Rajputs of this village were in all ways a particularly fine and gallant-looking lot of men, cheerful, courteous and well-mannered. Several of them, I was told, four or five anyway whom they named, were at that moment serving in the Army, and had, I suppose, been in that Kashmir contingent which had earned fame in the trying East African campaign—a change indeed from this mountain land to the swamps and morasses of the dark continent. The people of the village were poor, it was easy to see, with some few exceptions, but they bore themselves like men and gentlemen and showed a ready, but not officious, willingness to be helpful in every way. One little boy, with great solemn eyes, amused me by sitting opposite on the grass, after a grave salute, and staring at me steadily as I read. The turning of each page, I could see, was to him (as indeed it should be) like the opening of a new adventure. I regretted again (as I had often done in this country) that my ignorance of the dialect and the general ignorance of Hindustani among these people made communication next to impossible, except by an occasional smile.

One thing which is striking in these Kishtwari men is their headgear. They all, even those who have been converted to Islam, wear a cap which is in fact a replica of that usually worn by the Sanyasis or Hindu religious mendicants of India. A similar cap is also worn by the Son Kolis or fishermen of the Konkan coast near Bombay. But the Kolis know and can give the reason why they wear it, a commemoration of their conversion, some two hundred years ago, to the Hindu fold by such a religious mendicant, whose name they still revere. The Kishtwaris, however, who wear these caps of any colour and not merely of the dull scarlet which is the true insignia of the initiate, are unable to quote any tradition or assign any reason for the fashion. They are, indeed, as a whole, singularly uninformed of their own history or traditions. The women in Kishtwar, by the way, wear also a little cap, set coquettishly on the head, with just the slightest cock to one side, which is evidently from its shape a survival of the caps worn by the Mogul ladies of the great period in the Zananas of the Emperors at Delhi. The effect, with their cheap but plentiful jewelry set in hair and ears, in just the way that the Begums of those marble palaces wore their rich pearls and rubies, is to this day a curious reminiscence of those delicate, half-faded ivory miniatures of the Delhi capital, on which one may still scan with melancholy delight the fine eyes and pouting lips of the 'Destruction of the Palace' or 'The Light of the Universe.'

The night which I spent at Tugud was dreadful. A thunderstorm was gathering in the distance and the warm air was still and breathless. Mosquitoes moreover and gnats swarmed in thousands and bit and stung fiercely. Without even the covering of a sheet, in

Photograph by Vishinath of Shrinagar.

KISHTWARI WOMEN.

the thinnest of sleeping suits, I felt the oppression of the sultry air and sleep, when it came at last, was fitful and tormented.

Next morning we rose again before dawn, for the hottest of our marches was before us. Fortunately for me, a riding pony had been found in the village and I was only too glad to hire it for the next two marches. But after I had ridden a mile, the path became so rough that I had perforce to dismount and walk the next four miles. Then the path joined the main valley or gorge from Sinthan, where we met the main track between Kishtwar and Moghul Maidan. The day was still sultry and windless, with heavy thunder-clouds hanging upon the sky. Some rain, we found by the state of the road, had fallen a little further on, but it had not been enough to cool the air. It could only be the forerunner of other storms to come.

Moghul Maidan we passed as quickly as we could and pushed on another six miles to the depressing village of Chatru. Here we crossed the river, this time to the south, and entered the side nallah that was to lead us to the Girvit Pass into Kashmir. We went for another two miles up this nallah and I have seldom known any two miles so difficult to cover. It was already past the middle of the day and the sun had come out of the thunder-clouds at its fiercest. There was still no breath of wind and the temperature was that of India in the hot weather. Merely to exist was an exhaustion. A possible camping-place was at last found near a little mill beside the stream and we all lay down in such scanty shade as we could find. We had to stay like this for long and weary and finally for long and hungry hours, without even a bath or change of clothes. For it was nearly seven in the evening before the unfortunate coolies arrived with their burdens. We had started before seven in the morning and, measured by distance, the road was not more than fifteen miles in all. But the roughness of the track and above all, the unrelieved intensity of heat made it impossible even for the hardy hill-men to move more quickly. It was a weary camp that night and everyone went to sleep as soon as possible. Mosquitoes again made the night painful, yet, after Tugud, their mischief seemed almost tolerable. What annoyed me even more than the mosquitoes, however, was that I had developed prickly heat, an affection that I seldom feel even on the Indian plains in an Indian summer.

We started as early as usual on Sunday the 29th for Singpur, the last village on the Kishtwar side of the pass, where I had arranged to change transport coolies before starting to cross. The glen up which our path took us was really very beautiful, though the heat, which even at seven and eight in the morning was already excessive, detracted to some extent from one's appreciation. The luxuriance of vegetation was astonishing, grasses, flowers, bushes and trees all equally prolific and equally profuse. Among others it was a pleasure to see magnificent elms and to find ivy, the first I had seen for many years, clothing trunks and stones with its parasitic beauty.

At Singpur I found the village headman waiting for me with fresh coolies and sat down with him at the roadside till my transport could arrive. In the meantime I bought eggs and fowls for the next two days. While we were waiting, a party of three wandering musicians from Kashmir appeared on the scene. They had, they told me, crossed by the Sinthan pass—which they duly cursed—and were now moving on slowly from village to village in Kishtwar, getting food and a little money from the inhabitants and paying their way with Kashmiri melodies. They now sat down beside me on the village green and began to tinkle tunes from their drums and string instrument. Unfortunately they were not particularly brilliant as musicians, though they had been fine walkers. Even their time was erratic, an unusual fault in the East, and they misused one well-known Kashmiri song so badly, that in the end I simply had to interfere and beat the time for them for a few bars. But, good or indifferent, they were after all artists in their small way, and I felt I must give them *largesse* accordingly. For at the worst the poor artist —poor in either sense—is the interpreter of a spiritual universe which he adores as best he can and whose truth he confesses by his humblest efforts. At the worst he deserves that help and appreciation which is denied by any right-thinking man, not wholly without heart and soul, to the absurd tailor or candlestick-maker or boiler of fats and essences who acquires for himself the glorification of a sonorous peerage. A better and truer man by far is the most ruffianly gipsy fiddler that ever wrought flame and passion on the strings of a cracked violin from the notes of the Rakoczy March. With these Kashmiri mendicants of art I knew the touch of brotherhood and I crossed their palms with silver and gave them my blessing on their way. Let them wander on, poor fellows, through the mountains, giving to man and woman of their utmost the joys that they have, however thinly and feebly, learnt to create. Their reward will not be in wealth and external possessions and published honours and silent contempt. May they be rich instead, as artists, in the blessedness of the meek and humble of heart !

I now paid off my former coolies and bade them good-bye. The new men shouldered their loads and turned to the road and I started off again on the march to the pass. The owner of the pony which I had ridden, a decent Rajput with a pleasing sense of humour, who laughed and cracked jokes on the roughest path, now volunteered to come along with me as far as the pass, if I agreed to walk in the worst places. I felt that I was making a fatal concession to my natural laziness by consenting to ride further but, I thought, after all the day was hot and I knew the way was long. I did not hesitate another moment but closed with the offer gladly.

For the next four or five miles above Singpur the glen was even more beautiful than before, as we wound our way through noble forest at the side of a noisy stream. The ground and banks were thick with ferns and mosses, and the cold clear water raced round bends and curves and tossed over stones and little cascades. Yet, fine as it was, it could hardly be compared to the wondrous loveliness of the valley below the Sinthan pass. The path was anything but easy and the rivulet had to be crossed half-a-dozen times at least. Time after time I had to get off my pony and lead him over the rougher places. At the crossings, his Kishtwari owner, clothed simply in a loin-cloth and a small jacket, took the reins from my hand and nursed him carefully across the pools and rapids of the stream, while I found my tremulous way over the tree-trunks which took the place of bridges. There was one such crossing which was made up by placing four trees end to end, loosely poised on boulders, across a cascade—a horrible business.

But the worst part of the march was the last, a sharp upward heave and climb in a hot nallah for two miles or so above the tree line. I reached the slope where we were to spend the night by two in the afternoon, and the coolies arrived a couple of hours later with the kit. Straight above us we could see the bare summit of the Girvit Pass, something like one and a half hour's climb from our camp. The thunderstorm which had haunted us for two days was still following in our wake and it was matter for some anxiety whether or not it would catch us up that night. In itself a thunderstorm at that height and in so exposed a place would be none too pleasant. But, worst of all, heavy rain might well render the mountain crest impassable ; and, in any case, the extra weight of wet tents would probably be too much for the coolies at the gradient and elevation. A rainy night might, therefore, force us to stay an additional day or two on this bare patch of open hill-side, far from any possible supplies, till the sun came out again in force and our tents and kit could be dried.

With all these considerations in mind, everyone in the camp felt uneasy and many an anxious glance was cast by servants and master at the black clouds which were slowly covering the sky. The lowering storm made the air still and sultry and even at this height, 10,000 foot above sea-level, I could not bear a blanket during the night.

CHAPTER XVIII.

THE GIRVIT PASS—COMPARED TO THE SINTHAN PASS—A SNOW-BRIDGE—SINZAI VILLAGE—FISH AT WAYUL—CAMP AT KANDWARA.

HAPPILY for us, the rain which we had dreaded did not break that night when we were still on the Kishtwar side of the pass. But when we rose at dawn, the mountain was still shrouded in heavy cloud, and I felt we were lucky to escape.

The climb to the top of the pass was fairly steep but in no way troublesome or dangerous. I was able, in fact, to ride quite a considerable part of the way. Comparing the two routes to Kishtwar, the Sinthan pass by which I had entered and the Girvit pass by which I was leaving, I should on the whole recommend the latter for ease and comfort. The Sinthan pass, for one thing, is higher and more liable to interruption by snow. But the chief difference between the two routes is that the track by Sinthan had once been a road but has been allowed to fall into an appalling state of disrepair by apathy and neglect. *Corruptio optimi pessima*. Hence it is now in many places really dangerous and at the best is most fatiguing. Moreover, though it is meant for pony traffic, in its present condition it has become sheer cruelty to drag a horse over the so-called track.

The Girvit Pass, on the other hand, has no pretensions. It does not profess to be more than a footpath. The State administration has never meddled or marred. But constant use and the passing of many men has so far widened and levelled the little path that it is actually possible for ponies to cross. Their use is hardly to be advised, but I met quite a number coming down with light burdens, and, as I have said, I took a pony to the top on the Kishtwar side and was able to ride him for quite a considerable part of the way. Again the gradients are less steep than on the crest of the Sinthan pass ; the crossing can be completed in a shorter march ; there is not a single dangerous place to traverse ; and the risk of mountain-sickness is still smaller, as the height is less by eight hundred foot. On the Kashmir side the climb from the level of the Happy Valley to the bottom of the actual pass is very gentle and gradual. The only difficulty on the route is that the stream between Singpur and the pass has to be frequently crossed and re-crossed ; and the art of balancing oneself on a tree-trunk needs some learning by the stranger. The people of the country, I find, always use the Singpur route and the Girvit pass by preference to the dilapidated " high-road " over the Sinthan provided for them by the munificence of the State. But against all this additional comfort the traveller has to set one very material and preponderating fact, that the Sinthan route from the point of separation at Achabal all through till the tracks again join at Chatru is vastly superior in sheer loveliness. On the whole alternative route there is nothing to be compared in beauty to the constantly new but as constantly ravishing views afforded on the road from Dyusu and Rajpurtan across the Sinthan and down to Tsingam.

On the morning that I crossed the Girvit Pass the vale of Kashmir was fairly clear to the view but the clouds behind me were unfortunately too thick and low to admit of any last glance over Kishtwar. However, there was compensation in the spectacle close at hand; for the summit of the mountain was thickly covered with Alpine flowers. Five weeks before on the Sinthan pass, the dominant colour of the flowers had been blue. Now, with the progress of the season, or some difference in the soil, it was yellow. It was, perhaps, so much the less striking, for yellow blends too thoroughly with the green of grass to make its display as curiously impressive. On the Kashmir side of the crest, I found many bushes of the true Alpine rhododendron, but at this season they were of course not in flower.

We sat for some time on the top of the mountain and rested. My Rajput muleteer was now to return, so I passed him my cigarettes, and we chatted as we smoked. His name, he told me, was Bhima, like the hero of the Mahabharata. So I chaffed him and asked why he did not wield a mace like his legendary namesake; and he told me that he had a nephew, another Bhima, who had carried his rifle to East Africa in the war for his King and had won promotion in his regiment. Then we talked of the battles of Pandavs and Koravs in the legendary history of India; and we came again, by an easy transition, to the present war. He asked me the invariable question, which every one here asks, when the war was likely to end, and, like everyone else, hoped for our early and complete success. For the savage barbarity of the Germans has, by this time, penetrated to every remote recess of the Himalayas and is, I suppose, common talk in the uplands of Tibet and the encampments of wandering shepherds in Central Asia. Bestial cruelty and monstrous, inhuman deeds, the mark and ensign of the true Prussian beast, known long ago to all who know their Germany well, yet ignored till now, one cannot think why, by such multitudes, have at any rate reaped their harvest of universal and world-wide shame and disgrace. This earth is now linked and united by such quick transit and ready communication of thought and feeling as even a score of years ago would have been unimaginable ; and there is not left, in the most distant wilderness, one being of human form and mind, however ignorant, who does not bear his testimony to the eternal record of a whole people's degradation. East to West, and North to South there is no hamlet so small, no tribe so wild and primitive, that the name of German does not rouse a shudder, as of some indelible horror stamped upon the shape of man.

We said good-bye at last and parted, and I went down the path to the well-known valley of Kashmir. For the first thousand foot the descent was fairly steep to a nallah that had to be crossed on a snow-bridge or moraine about fifty or sixty yards across. Thence forward it was all easy-going, a gradual steady descent down the Marbal glen. I had breakfast on the road at Karbudrun meadow, a favourite camping-place for

Gujjars, and pushed on again to the bottom of the Marbal glen where it runs at right angles into the wider valley of the Aro river. Here we cut a corner and saved a *détour* by following a sheep-track on the face of the hill, till we descended again on the further side into the valley. We could now see in front of us the village of Sinzai, where we were to spend the night. By this time I was of course far in advance of our transport-coolies. So I lay down to wait for them in a convenient field, beside water, under the shade of a spreading walnut. The sun was hot, but all the way down the glen we had been met by the pleasant and tempered breezes of Kashmir, which so seldom fail the inhabitants of that favoured country and which were in delightful contrast to the still fierce heat of the Kishtwar gorges. The coolies followed sooner than I expected and by three o'clock the tents were pitched in the village of Sinzai, on a spot that was one-third apple orchard and two-thirds graveyard. For no one in Kashmir seems to mind the most familiar usage of their God's acres, and, as my *shikari* said with much sense, "the dead after all could not harm us." Here men do not think that the presence of the living is a disrespect to those who lie under the grass waiting for the trump of resurrection. They plant gorgeous irises upon the graves of the dead and leave the rest to the care of mother earth.

The next morning saw us further on our way into the heart of Kashmir. We passed on our right at Gonda, the picturesque shrine of Baba Daud, perched on the side of a hill, where it dominates with its tapering spire the shaded depths of two valleys. The saint whose memory is here perpetuated seems by repute to be vouchsafed power over atmospheric pressures, storm currents and the like. For his intercession is required by deputations with rustic offerings whenever there is fear of drought or excessive rain or any kindred calamity to the crops. Fortunately, as the climate of Kashmir is as variable as the English, the request for his use of these cyclonic or anti-cyclonic powers is never likely to be long infructuous.

A short way on, at Wayul, there are a couple of pools in the river so wonderfully thronged with fish, that numbers might be caught by a single cast of a net. The place is a favourite with those sportsmen who like to take their fish easily. It was fascinating to look over the bridge and see hundreds of fish in the clear water lying packed side by side or moving lazily and snapping at the insects on the surface.

Here at Wayul the small valley from Sinzai meets the larger valley of the river Bring at right angles, and a little further on is the considerable village of Wangam. I enquired here about bear, and was told that some other Saheb had beat the small patches of forest near the village two days before, that there had been a bear and that the Saheb had missed. It was obviously no use to try the same beats again so soon after the bear had been fired at. We, therefore, walked on to Sop, another large village five miles beyond on the other side of the valley. My *shikari* had hopes of hearing authentic news of bear here, as he had friends in the village. But, when we got to Sop, we found only vague reports of bear and nothing exact or accurate. Near the village it was definitely stated that no bear had been seen but there was some hope in a forest some distance away and high above human habitations. But on mere vague hopes and possibilities it seemed hardly worth the trouble of a long climb. I decided, therefore to push on another two and a half miles to the next village of Kandwara, from which we had already had detailed and hopeful information.

The road between Sop and Kandwara was very unpleasant. The path lay along a river bed, all a mass of stones, difficult to walk on, with no protection against the sun, and with the stream to wade through four times. The day had been sultry and oppressive since morning, for the thunderstorm we had left in Kishtwar was again pursuing us ; and the sun was blazing through the humid air as we picked our way in the full glare reflected from the stones. Happily we found a very shady place for our camp at Kandwara under a couple of large walnut-trees. It was too near the village and was surrounded by rice-fields, always a serious disadvantage. But the shade at any rate was grateful. We had walked fifteen miles from Sinzai in great heat and it was enjoyable to rest in the opaque shadows cast by the fine trees.

In the late afternoon, however, I roused myself to go with my *shikari* and a couple of villagers and climb up a nallah to the hill-side above some maize-fields which a bear had that night entered and damaged. The slopes were fortunately of the usual gentle Kashmir gradients, very different from the sudden heights of Kishtwar.

The sides of the hill were covered with barberry bushes, their blue-black berries now ripened in the summer-heat, and we ate freely, as we went up, of the rather acrid but refreshing little fruit. We sat down on a convenient rock in the hope of intercepting the bear on his way down from the hill-top to the maize-fields. But it shortly began to rain, at first gently and then with greater force, while not far away we could watch a heavier thunderstorm passing from the Kishtwar road and the Wardwan valley across the Liddar and Pahlgam to the city of Srinagar. In this rain, it was not likely that the bear would prowl and, after enduring the wet till eight o'clock, I gave up the attempt and returned to my camp and a bath and change of clothes, having added another three miles to the distance I had walked that day.

CHAPTER XIX.

TWO DAYS' BEATS—RETURN TO KANBAL—BACK IN THE HOUSE-BOAT.

I HAD settled to devote the next day, the 1st of August, to beating for bear in the neighbouring forests. Above Kandwara the hills are low and for the most part treeless. But in places there are small strips of forest running up and down the hill-side. These can be easily and thoroughly driven and afford a home for bear at the right season. On the other side of the range, however, lies the large game reserve or *rukh* of Achabal, and, as it has now become the natural resort of those animals, it is on any given day a question of doubt whether any bear has, after his night meal in the peasants' fields, remained in the strips of village forest or has moved back over the top to the reserve.

But on this occasion all were hopeful, as a bear had in the night visited a field on the further side of a ridge which I had contemplated as I sat up the previous evening. This field was immediately below one of the most likely of the forest patches. Moreover, as I came to the place fixed for the first beat, I could see fresh foot-marks and hoped, therefore, that the animal had not gone much further. The place where I sat was the highest point of a wood that covered both sides of a nallah, and the beaters came up through the wood from the bottom, taking good care to throw out moving 'stops' on both wings. The beat was beautifully done, the men working in perfect line and order, cheered on by the music of two drums and a sort of harsher and more strident clarionet called a '*surnai.*' But all the same it was a blank and it was clear that the bear could not have spent his sleeping hours in this forest. He must have moved on either to the other strips of wood we were now to beat or, as I feared, across the crest of the hill to the reserve. But the following two beats, one of which was in a wood curiously reminiscent of Indian jungle and a panther's lair, were equally without result, though this ill-success was in no way due to the beaters. They had worked without a single fault.

When all was over, I ate my luncheon in the forest, and the men brought me some raspberries and wild apples. The last were quite new to me. They were yellow in colour and very small, not more than an inch and a half in diameter. They were, however, very sweet and pleasant, and were rather of the "mealy" than the hard type of apple. As I smoked after luncheon, the men talked. Like all Kashmiris they were keenly interested in the war and very patriotic. The Kashmiris have of course suffered severely in pocket by the war, for the usual stream of officers on leave has for two years been diverted and even this year is much smaller in volume than in the former days of peace. To do them justice, however, it must also be said that their interest is by no means solely or perhaps even mainly based on pecuniary interests. Most of the *shikaris* and the professional shooting coolies, even many of the villagers, had friends among the English officers that came here whom they remember with respect and affection. Of those they recall many who have been killed, many others whom, on account of wounds and illness, they shall never again see in these mountains. And further, they have acquaintances and some few of them have relations in the Kashmir regiments at the front and feel a natural and very proper pride in their successes and the medals and honours won by the men of their own glens and mountains. Hence the constant question to every Englishman they meet is of the war and its duration, and they eagerly drink in every description of the fighting which one can give them. Their main difficulty, of course, is to understand the immobility of trench warfare and it is this to them unintelligible and incalculable stationariness which, if anything, leads them at times to despondency. It would be well worth while, I should think, for the Kashmir Government to arrange, as was so successfully done at least at the beginning of the war in India, for popular lectures in which the principal features of this campaigning should be explained and illustrated. I did my best to explain the length of the western front, the reasons for its slow yielding, and the main issue in this war of nations of relative mass and rapidity of destruction ; and I found that the men followed my explanation with care and, I think, with some resulting mental image not too inappropriate to the reality. Perhaps their most actual interest, however, was in the aeroplanes, which they had not yet seen and which they could only figure as something portentous, even miraculous.

I was amused, also, after the subject of the war was, if not exhausted, at any rate for the moment laid aside to find these villagers inquisitive and eager about the properties, for health and taste, of tea and coffee, and their prices in England and in India. Tea is, of course, a staple with the Kashmiri, though he usually drinks it mixed with salt : and far better tea is to be obtained in every bazar in Kashmir, than can be found except by hard search in the largest town of India. But coffee has only very lately been known in the country and even the Mussulman population has not yet learnt to serve small cups of coffee at their festivals and meetings like their co-religionists in the plains. My *shikari* then went on to ask me about chocolate, from what it is made and how it is produced and its special properties, as he had noticed that I usually drank chocolate in the morning by preference to stimulants like tea and coffee, and did so always when I was going out for a long and tiring day on the hills or on the march. This lively curiosity is certainly one of the most hopeful qualities of the Kashmiri people. That their minds are as a rule quick and active, there can be no doubt ; and when at last education or at any rate literacy is forced to the door of every man, and the existing shackles of superstition are thereby shattered, I cannot but believe that the vivid intelligence of this people will play a leading part in the development both of Indian and of Central Asian thought. In the meantime, unhappily, they remain mentally stunted and deformed by the pressure of a determined obscurantism. It is this obscurantism, on which certain parasitic classes of the community build their authority and their unearned wealth, which is responsible for the worst of all the curses that afflict the prostrate land, its universal and appalling dirt. The dirt is such that its like cannot be paralleled in the whole length and breadth of modern India. But here the very name of science is countered and traduced by the vociferous advocates of superstition and a guilty self-interest; and the filthiest practices are enjoined and recommended under sanctified pretensions. The drinking of the mortally disgusting river water, for instance, water quite unspeakably polluted and palpably malodorous, is countenanced by those who would protect faith against human knowledge, though it is without doubt the main cause of an excessive infant mortality which even in this wonderful natural sanatorium tells each year of the extinction in dirt of tens of thousands of the innocents. *Tantum potnit suadere malorum relligio.* But here in Kashmir the Englishman, coming on a passing visit, sees with his eyes open, in the moral conditions which invite his observation. He sees the evil and can read its cause. But in our own land where we look with a gaze habituated to our surroundings and thereby inobservant and uninterested, can we say that the ills of obscurantism have finally been suppressed? Here, at any rate, in Kashmir is warning enough for any man.

I spent the next day again in abortive beats above Kandwara and the adjoining village of Akingam. In one beat a fox ran out; and in another a sounder of pig, two sows and a half-a-dozen piglets. But no bear presented himself to my rifle. Gamblers have a saying that the cards never forgive and so, I suppose, it must be with sport. I had had my chance at a bear on Pahlma and had lost it by wishing it to be better. Now, I seemed to be in for a run of bad luck. The excessive heat, I presumed more scientifically, must be driving the bears to spend their days in the deeply wooded and shady reserve on the other side of the mountain. I, therefore, thought it hopeless to waste time on any more attempts, especially since the effort was tiring and unpleasant in the exceptional heat-wave. Better luck, I hoped, might be mine when I again started shooting in September. In the meantime, the best thing was to break off and return to our boat on the river.

I left accordingly for Kanbal next morning, a dull march of thirteen miles, in very still and hot weather, over country which was plain and homely. Here I paid off my attendants, except the *shikari*, Muhammad Ganai, whose services I was retaining for September. With one exception all had worked very well and I thanked them for their performance of their duties with genuine sincerity. But one ruffian among them, the cook, I left behind with almost frantic joy. For six weeks I had been this malevolent butcher's prey, and there had been days when I had nearly starved at his hands and had had to sustain myself on maize-bread cooked by the *shikari*. He was the villain of our little piece and I should have liked to have hastened his exit with some of the eggs and vegetables he himself had made uneatable by his cooking. But this might have been too cruel a punishment and I let him go in peace with his ill-gotten shekels.

My wife, who, of course, did not expect me till the 5th of August, had not yet brought our boat to Kanbal, so, after breakfast, I hired a country craft for myself and my belongings and started down the river to look for her, where I thought she would still be, in the beautiful camp at Bijbehara. But I met her in the boat coming up half-an-hour later and thereby brought my little trip to its close. It was pleasant to put on civilized clothes again after all those weeks and I delighted in the feel of a stiff collar at my neck.